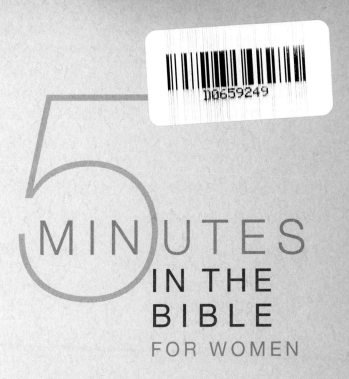

5 MINUTES
IN THE
BIBLE
FOR WOMEN

EMILIE BARNES

HARVEST HOUSE PUBLISHERS
EUGENE, OREGON

Cover design by Koechel Peterson & Associates Inc., Minneapolis, Minnesota

Cover photo © Thinkstock

FIVE MINUTES IN THE BIBLE FOR WOMEN
Copyright © 2015 Emilie Barnes
Published by Harvest House Publishers
Eugene, Oregon 97402
www.harvesthousepublishers.com

Library of Congress Cataloging-in-Publication Data
　　Barnes, Emilie.
　　Five minutes in the Bible for women / Emilie Barnes.
　　　　Pages cm
　　ISBN 978-0-7369-6142-4 (pbk.)
　　ISBN 978-0-7369-6143-1 (eBook)
　　1. Women—Prayers and devotions. 2. Bible—Devotional literature. I. Title.
　　BV4844.B355 2015
　　242'.643—dc23

　　　　　　　　　　　　　　　　　　　　　　　　2015015049

Printed in the United States of America

15 16 17 18 19 20 21 22 23 / BP-JH / 10 9 8 7 6 5 4 3 2 1

To seven of my most enduring women friends.
You have given me great legacy moments
in the past and in the present, and you certainly will in the future.
You are women who give me real purpose in life.

Jenny Whitney
(my daughter)

Christine Ianni
(Jenny's daughter; my first granddaughter)

Emi Ianni
(Christine's daughter; my first great-granddaughter)

Stephanie Barnes
(wife of my son, Brad)

Erica Merrihew
(wife of my first grandson, Chad)

Lucy May Merrihew
(daughter of Chad and Erica; my second great-granddaughter)

Erica Merrihew
(wife of my second grandson, Bevan)

God has blessed me with you, such dear, godly women
who want to know and apply biblical principles in your lives.
Long after I'm gone to be with the Lord,
I know you will carry on the traditions of our faith.

A Note from Emilie

Time is such a big factor in our lives. All of us are struggling to fit everything we have to do into twenty-four-hour segments of time. The stresses and burdens of that struggle are not what God wants for us. If you examine your biggest worries, chances are they're tied to actions or choices that you've made a priority rather than being tied to requests God has made in your life. That's why I've learned to say "No" to good things and save my "Yes" for the best.

While doing this, I've established priorities for what needs to be done and relates to what really matters most in my life. One of my prized choices has been to give some valuable time each day to reading materials that will help me grow in my faith. In addition to reading the Bible, I've found it helpful to have resources that encourage the habit of daily reflection and understanding. I pray this book will be that kind of companion for you in your quiet time.

Giving God five minutes a day is not asking too much! Yet, it does take intention and practice to turn this into a regular part of your routine. When I make this time with God a regular morning routine, I find I have a much better day. I feel more connected to God's heart and will, I accomplish more of what I need to get done, and I am more sensitive to taking moments to pray and be still before Him. It takes twenty-one days to form a new habit in life. Why not start developing this new habit of spending five minutes with God daily?

May you be blessed as you read through these short, daily thoughts.

Emilie Barnes

*All Scripture is God-breathed and is useful for
teaching, rebuking, correcting and training in righteousness,
so that the servant of God may be thoroughly
equipped for every good work.*

2 Timothy 3:16-17

Begin Each Day with God

*Watch therefore, for you know neither the
day nor the hour in which the Son of Man
is coming (Matthew 25:13 NKJV).*

It takes twenty-one consecutive days to form a new habit. If you aren't used to starting the day off with God, today will be your first day. Only twenty more days and you'll have a new routine. That length of time helps you to impress on your life this added priority.

I've found that the most amazing infusions of God's strength happen when I'm taking the risk of obeying God. I'm astonished at how my Lord can take my tiny step of faith and turn it into a strong leap for His kingdom.

You may be a mom whose teenagers are in trouble. You may be struggling with an illness or working at a job that saps your spirit. Whatever set of circumstances you face today, purpose in your heart and daily routine to hear the voice of God through reading Scripture and praying each day before heading off to the events that face you.

We need to exercise our faith by turning to God when life seems too much. The Bible tells us the truth about these circumstances. We may be weak, but He is strong. His arms are extending to you and all your troubles. He is also there during your periods of praise. As a mom you love to hear "Thank you" from your children—and so does God.

All you have to do is be still and take a few minutes to hear what He has to say to you. God is not to be considered your Santa Claus. He isn't waiting for your shopping list, but He does want to hear about your hopes and needs. He isn't to be used as a fire extinguisher, only reached for when troubles are burning out of control. He wants you to reach for Him every day—and when you have praises too!

He is your Father in heaven, and He longs to spend time with you. As you turn to Him faithfully and this new habit becomes an integral part of your life's rhythm, you'll become more motivated to go to God with everything going on. And you'll inspire your family and others to do the same.

Father God, before I get busy with another day, I want to spend time with You. Our communication will help my attitude before I engage with the world and remind me of Your love and available wisdom. How grateful I am that I can come to You anytime and know You care about what I have to say...and You care about what You have to share with me. Amen.

Take Action

Start your journey toward developing a habit of prayer and praise today. If you don't know where to begin, I suggest the book of Proverbs. And make *Five Minutes in the Bible for Women* part of your journey. Together we can move you toward a great new habit.

Your Reflections

_____

_____

_____

Get More from Your Bible Reading

*The Advocate, the Holy Spirit, whom the Father will
send in my name, will teach you all things and will
remind you of everything I have said to you (John 14:26).*

There is much to gain, learn from, and reflect on in the Bible. In order to glean as much of God's message for you and to take it to heart, you might want to consider the following steps as guidelines for your reading time. I believe they'll help you as you venture out on this journey of spending time in the Word.

First, pick a book of the Bible to read. For each chapter ask these questions and write out your answers.

1. *What is this chapter in this book about?* Through your reading, get a general overview of what the author is saying. What is the main message?

2. *What does this chapter teach about God/Jesus/Holy Spirit?* Now go back again and read more slowly with the thought of searching for this specific answer.

3. *What sin is there to confess, and what is a behavior or belief to avoid?* The writer is usually teaching a specific principle concerning the Christian walk.

4. *What example is there to follow?* To get this answer, you might need to reread the selection several times. What step in your Christian walk might this scripture be suggesting you take?

5. *What command is there to obey?* The Bible doesn't give "maybes" or "suggestions." The writers are usually direct in delivering God's messages.

6. *What promise is there to believe and trust in?* If you search hard enough, you'll find the needle in the haystack.

7. *What is my favorite verse in this book?* I encourage you to write it on an index card and memorize it this week. Include why it's special to you. You'll be amazed at all the riches you'll gather over time.

8. *What does this book communicate to me?* Pray for guidance and help in understanding what God is saying to you. As you read through the chapter, *listen* carefully for His message. Thank Him for speaking to you as you ask for His help to change.

Father God, give me the desire to follow these simple steps to better understand Your Word and be patient as I dive deeper into the heart of Your messages. Open my eyes so I can see how Your truths and wisdom can become my foundation for daily living. Help me draw closer to You as I grow in You. Amen.

Take Action

Choose a portion of Scripture to read and ask these questions. As you begin, go through the guidelines twice so addressing the questions becomes a natural process.

Your Reflections

_____

_____

_____

God's Peace in Our Insecure World

*Lazy people want much but get little, but those
who work hard will prosper (Proverbs 13:4 NLT).*

Everyone is talking about security these days. We want it, but we don't always want the structure and restrictions that come with security measures. We can see human efforts to create security in our airports and in our neighborhoods. In Southern California, many of the new housing communities are constructed behind fences or walls with guard gates to pass through for entry. And there are often security guards who patrol the streets and check up on those who do go through the gates.

So many people are saying they don't feel safe anymore, even with these extra measures. I believe our "default" mode is to pursue the worldly ways to feel safe and protected. Most folks are looking for more ways to separate themselves from potential physical harm and destruction. It isn't surprising that those physical measures do little to ease their restless hearts and minds.

As believers in Jesus Christ, we can take the secure path to God's heart and His sanctuary. We can surrender to Him in spirit. As Christians, we can know and enjoy the peace of God in this insecure world. When we're diligent and work hard to grow our faith, the result is a deep knowing of God's rest and care. My husband, Bob, and I know from our difficult walk through my cancer journey that God can give us peace beyond all human understanding.

I believe God has a record of all my prayers and His answers. I need to remember that even on those days when God seems far away, His peace is nearby and available. As you and I awaken each morning, we can be assured that our heavenly Father will be the same today as the one before. Our God is never too busy to hear from us. There are no busy signals, voice-mail messages, or disconnections when we call on the Lord Jesus Christ.

Father God, may I enter Your peace today with joy. Help me trust You with my life, my marriage, my family, and my possessions. You shepherd me through uncertain valleys, and You bring me back to Your path when I've lost my way. Thank You for always hearing my calls and for never leaving me behind. Amen.

Take Action

Think about the ways you've tried to create physical and financial security in your life. Now think about the ways you want to start investing in *spiritual* security...by growing your faith in the Lord.

Your Reflections

_____

_____

_____

Developing a Life of Faith

*"Abraham believed God, and it was credited
to him as righteousness," and he was
called God's friend (James 2:23).*

Wow! Abraham must have been a great man to be a friend of God. I
would certainly like to be in that circle of friends. But wait…*I am!*
Not only am I a friend of God's, but I am a child of His too. My hope
is that I will be considered a person of great faith just as Abraham was.

Throughout his life, Abraham exhibited his strong faith in God.
He learned that God would provide, and his dependence on and faith
in God grew. You and I probably won't have the same challenges facing us in life that Abraham did, but the same principles are applica-
ble for our successes in life. We are to know that God will provide. In
Hebrews 11:8-9, two words that stand out are "by faith":

> *By faith* Abraham, when called to go to a place he would
> later receive as his inheritance, obeyed and went, even
> though he did not know where he was going. *By faith* he
> made his home in the promised land like a stranger in a
> foreign country; he lived in tents, as did Isaac and Jacob,
> who were heirs with him of the same promise.

In most situations Abraham encountered, he applied this basic
principle of living a life of faith: God will provide. In order for us to
live lives that are worthy to follow, we must leave a legacy that shows
to the people watching us that we truly believe God will provide.

What are we going to put on our altars of life? Our families, our
jobs, our homes, our possessions? On and on, each day we worry

about what we have and want. Why do we worry so much? One Barnes family motto is "God is good *all* the time." And I believe this with all of my heart. I've witnessed His mercy and goodness throughout my lifetime, and I've spoken with countless women who also have been blessed to be witnesses of God's great grace and love.

If we really believe that God will provide, then why do we invest so much of ourselves into things that don't have eternal value or lead us into His peace? Let's shift our perspectives so we're living by faith and not by fear or so we are living by faith and not by unfocused, unintentional choices.

Father God, give me Your discernment to demonstrate to those around me that I truly believe You will provide. Give me the courage to live by faith in You. Amen.

Take Action

By faith, trust God to provide for a specific need you have. Lift up that need today in prayer.

Your Reflections

_____

_____

_____

Make a Joyful Sound

Rejoice in the Lord always. I will say it
again: Rejoice! (Philippians 4:4).

As believers in the hope given to us in and by Scripture, we can rejoice even in difficult times. Rejoicing doesn't depend on our circumstances. That doesn't mean we're always smiling, but our hearts and spirits can hold to an attitude of rejoicing. Paul was in prison when he wrote today's encouragement to the believers in Jesus Christ in Philippi. Think about that. From the darkest, bleakest human place he could be in, Paul was able to speak with joy and light.

I read about a couple living in England during the bombing of London in World War II. They were also able to rejoice even during the difficult years. Once this joyful couple was overheard laughing by a cynical neighbor who asked, "What on earth are you two laughing about?" The woman's voice and facial expression reflected disbelief and even anger. The problem is illuminated within her question. She asked "what on *earth*" the couple was finding to laugh about during that very troubling time in history and their lives. The couple was finding their joy *in heaven* and *in God's presence*. It was the hope He gives that can overrule hardship. Do you see what a shift that is? The world focuses on earthly troubles, but believers are given eyes, and minds, and hearts that can focus on the treasures and wisdom from heaven. No wonder so many people in the world can't figure Christians out.

How can we seem to be undisturbed during tough times? This kind of tough love can irritate many who don't feel it or have it or know how it comes about. Rather than rejoicing with us or asking us about it, often they choose to scoff.

Laypeople say it's okay to rejoice when we have some concrete reason for it, such as when we win the lotto or we get a raise in pay at work. But if we have no obvious reason for our joy, we're likely to be looked upon as being a bit strange. The Bible tells us that joy is not just for the good times. It's for *all* times. To be able to live in a continual state of joy, we must walk in the Holy Spirit. We must also look for what God is teaching us through our current circumstances. Consider what lessons in joy and trust you can learn today.

Dear Lord, I want to have the joy that Paul talked about even while he was in prison. I don't want to just be joyful during the good circumstances of life. I know You are with me during all the ups and downs. Help me to lean into Your safe presence always. Amen.

Take Action

Sing a song of praise to God or play a favorite inspirational song. Let your spirit soar to Him.

Your Reflections

_____

_____

_____

Where There Is Hope, There Is Life

But now, Lord, what do I look for? My
hope is in you (Psalm 39:7).

The word "hope" is used often in Scripture. It holds great value in the Christian life. We might get the impression from casual conversations or greeting cards that hope is like a wish, but it's much stronger than that. When our hope is in Christ, it is rooted in His strength, His power, and His promises.

You know the old saying, "Where there's life, there's hope"? I would like to put it differently. I'd say, "Without hope, life as we know it is simply impossible." How can we survive without at least a tiny spark of possibility? How can we thrive without a healthy sense of promise? How can we grow unless hope keeps us looking and learning and moving forward? I believe that's what hope really is. It's the desire and ability to move forward in God's grace and power.

One of the great moments of contrast in life is the experience we have when attending a funeral service. If it is services for nonbelievers, the sentiment surrounding the time is focused on loss and grief. They lived, they died, and that's it. There's not much joy in that type of service.

But when you attend a celebration for a person of faith, you hear a lot of stories that project hope in an eternal life. The memorial service gives us an awareness that there's more to life than the grave. Someday we believers will be joined together in heaven—that's our assurance. Hope is an interest and investment in tomorrow. It guides us when we encounter times of sorrow or pain.

When normal life is spinning merrily along, we need that sense of possibility to keep the day-to-day stresses of home and/or office from wearing us down. When life crashes and burns, such as when sickness strikes...or a pink slip arrives...or a friend lets us down...or we just seem to lose the way, we need hope as a lifeline to pull us through and keep us going toward better times. We need a hope that is stronger than death. And, my friend, we have that in Jesus.

Father God, I find that Your Word gives me hope for the future. It helps me trust that hope in You conquers the pain of anything that might unfold, even the sting of death. I've been let down by people, but never by You. When I face my dark times, I know I can come to You with my hurts and my failings, and You will receive me in love. You will guide me toward a more fulfilling life in You. Amen.

Take Action

Where is your hope found? In death and the grave or in the hope of eternity in your soul? Evaluate the choice. What do you need to do right now?

Your Reflections

_____

_____

_____

I'd Rather Be Rich

*Let no debt remain outstanding, except the
continuing debt to love one another, for whoever
loves others has fulfilled the law (Romans 13:8).*

I laugh when I hear the line "I've been rich and I've been poor—rich is better." Of course, most of us would agree. Yet for the Christian, the only reason to be rich is to have resources to help carry out God's plan while we're here on earth. God certainly doesn't need our wealth, and He doesn't need our possessions. But we need to give our time and money to Him.

When we lovingly and obediently fulfill our role as givers (regardless of how much we have to give), God will use these offerings to minister to others. Often it is our willingness to give that opens the floodgates for more giving. We realize why it is important and see God at work, so we're inclined to give even more. And when other people see our example, they too might be inspired to give and give again. One small gesture can become a large movement of compassion and kindness.

We all know how good it feels to give, so I find it interesting how many people don't build giving into their family budget. It should be at the top of the list. Giving to God should always be first. We carry out this objective not only by tithing but by giving, as He leads us, to our families, our communities, and even to strangers. Don't get caught up in thinking, "When we have this or that or make this much, we'll start giving." It won't happen. We never have "enough." We need to create our habits for giving now. And we certainly are modeling for our children and others how to give.

Everything you have belongs to God. Giving back to Him should happen no matter what our income or circumstances. Not only are we to give our money, but also our time and attention. The ultimate outcomes are that God will be pleased and we will be blessed.

> Father God, I want to develop a way of life that is focused on giv-ing back to You all that You have given to me. Help me be wise and in balance as I provide and care for my family and reach out to others. Release my hold on possessions, and time, and income so that I will freely direct those resources in the way You guide me to. I want to seek You in all my decisions. Amen.

Take Action

Spend time with your family and review your goals for giving back to God what He has so richly given you. Ask members of your family how they want to use their talents and gifts to honor God.

Your Reflections

_____

_____

_____

Lessons Not Learned in School

*A wise man will hear and increase in
learning, and a man of understanding will
acquire wise counsel (Proverbs 1:5 NASB).*

Have you ever frozen when you faced an important decision? Or lost your focus in the midst of lots of opinions and perspectives? I definitely have. When this happens, nothing is accomplished, and we become too weary to learn and grow.

There are ways we can create a strong foundation of wisdom for ourselves and our children and grandchildren. We all know that most important lessons aren't found in a typical textbook, so it's of great importance to gather together and then teach these bits of wisdom to younger generations. Here are a few particular lessons that go far beyond the classroom knowledge:

1. *Don't do everything yourself.* While being independent has its benefits, be sure you don't take this to an extreme. Leaning on God's strength for life situations is essential. When we refuse help, we are limiting how God can work in and through others and ourselves.

2. *Make your efforts count.* Keep trying. Many very successful people weren't successful the first time or even a few times after that. Investing in preparation for any endeavor does pay off because the opportunity will not have been wasted—even if it doesn't turn out as planned. This is a wonderful lesson to pass along to younger generations. How often have we heard (or even said), "What's the use?" We won't grow if we

aren't willing to put more behind an effort than just words or wishes. Prayer and intentional work shape lasting habits with eternal benefits.

3. *Have a good attitude.* Approach your work, family, and relationships with joy and gratitude. This will change the way you receive and handle glitches that interfere with your plans.

4. *Be a woman with integrity.* An honest woman with trustworthy character is a success. If you mentor a young person, model integrity at all times. This doesn't mean you have to be perfect! It means that in every circumstance you do your best to follow and represent God.

Lord, let me always be a learner who is dependable and trustworthy at work and at home. Give me a heart that seeks to unite and build bridges so that I serve and build up others. Amen.

Take Action

Evaluate how you are doing in the areas we just looked at. How well are you passing them along to others? Plan a specific day to pay special attention to each one of these actions. In your journal, note how it changes your perspective and how it might change the responses of others to you.

Your Reflections

_____

_____

_____

Financial Responsibility Is Financial Freedom

To the person who pleases him, God gives wisdom,
knowledge and happiness (Ecclesiastes 2:26).

Are you someone who just can't pass up a good deal? When you see something at a discount price, does that item all of a sudden become a need or priority for you? Sometimes a good deal isn't nearly as valuable as a good idea. If we are immersed in God's Word and conversation with Him through prayer, we are more likely to discern and follow His wisdom and leading. And, with God's help, we'll keep learning every year of our lives, especially about the importance of being responsible with the blessings we are given.

You can manage your money even better when you have a spiritual purpose for your life. If your spiritual purpose is to serve God, all your resources minister toward that end. If a "good deal" has been your budget's downfall, you now have a way to measure the worth of that sale item. There is always a battle between "want" and "need." Ask yourself if something you're considering buying or a pursuit you're planning serves your spiritual mission or provides for the ministry of your family and friends in a necessary way.

Keep in mind that *the goal of financial responsibility is financial freedom*. I know it can be difficult to say "No" to some things now in order to gain freedom later. Let's face it, our culture is geared more toward immediate gratification. But if your mind and goals are set on God's best, then these decisions do become easier. I promise.

Be content with your present income level. Make regular giving a family priority. Pay your debts as they fall due. Recognize that God owns everything; everything is only on loan to you. Your home, your car, your marriage, your children, your job—everything. You may use them, love them, benefit from them, but you don't own them and they aren't rights. God said, "The silver is mine and the gold is mine" (Haggai 2:8). Use God's resources wisely.

> Father God, I want to be rich in spirit. I want my money to serve a spiritual purpose. Help me be discerning in my heart and in my financial choices when the "bargains" of the world appear. Give me a generosity of spirit so that my hands never hold on to possessions and my heart never holds back from showing Your love to others. Amen.

Take Action

Review with your family some areas in your financial life that need attention. Your goal is to have financial freedom so you have the freedom to give as God leads you to give.

Your Reflections

_____

_____

_____

Principles for Giving

*Each of you should give what you have decided in your
heart to give, not reluctantly or under compulsion,
for God loves a cheerful giver (2 Corinthians 9:7).*

People always are asking me, "How much money must I give to be
a good Christian?" In 2 Corinthians 9, the apostle Paul inspires the
believers in Corinth, along with you and me, regarding the principles of giving:

1. *You reap what you sow* (verse 6). This is a farming principle.
   In order to get a future crop, we can't cheat when it comes
   to planting plenty of seeds. When we give very little, we
   receive very little. People who are stingy with resources or in
   the giving of their time and attention aren't investing in the
   harvest they'll want later. Meanwhile, there are people who
   have very few resources but give as often as God leads them
   to give. They will have an abundant harvest in what matters.
   Think of the joy, and love, and sense of community that take
   root and sprout when we give.

2. *Be a cheerful giver* (verse 7). Don't give out of pressure, but
   give freely and joyfully because you want to express God's
   heart to others, expand His ministry, and be His obedient
   servant in all parts of your life.

This all sounds doable, right? Then why is it so difficult for us to
walk in these principles sometimes? I believe that we become fearful
about our own security, and then we forget the great privilege it is to
join with God and be His hands and His help to many.

My friend, you'll be blessed in your obedience. Only after we give are we ready to fully receive what God has for us. We'll know and feel His love even more when we're cheerful givers. In fact, when we do extend any part of ourselves or our possessions to others, that is probably when we best understand God's nature. Each time we give to God and His work through our local churches, Christian ministries throughout the world, and to individuals, we're practicing godly stewardship. We are accepting from God our personal responsibility for what He's given.

Women carry a lot of responsibilities. We most definitely do! So remember that life isn't about achieving a specific level of giving or a level of financial well-being so that we can give from a place of plenty. The surrendering of our hearts and our offerings to God, no matter the amount we have to give, are considered great treasures.

Don't ever doubt the value of yourself or of what you have to give to God.

> Father God, let me examine my priorities for giving. Do I willingly contribute or do I hesitate in my giving? Help me be a cheerful giver. Amen.

Take Action

Get to the point where you give because you want to, not because you feel pressured to give.

Your Reflections

_____

_____

_____

Be in Agreement with God

So do not worry, saying, "What shall we eat?" or "What shall we drink?" or "What shall we wear?"...Seek first his kingdom and his righteousness, and all these things will be given to you as well (Matthew 6:31,33).

This is one of my very favorite passages of Scripture. When we come to a fork in the road and aren't sure what direction we should go, we can come back to this verse. Which decision would be most pleasing to God? Why do we need this? Why do we ask God's leading in this decision? God's will for a person's life is a lifelong endeavor that takes years of reading the Word, searching the Word, and praying to grow in pleasing God in our daily lives.

We are so used to reading disclaimers when buying products. There will be tags or instructions that come with them. These explain how to use their product properly. It's the same way with prayer. The great theologian Charles Spurgeon always added this disclaimer to his prayers:

> Lord, if I have asked for anything that is not according to Your mind, I ask You to disregard it. And if any wish that I have expressed to You—even though it is the desire that burns in my bosom above all other wishes—is a wish that is not right in Your sight, disregard it, my Father. But in Your infinite love and compassion, do something better for Your servant than Your servant knows how to ask.

What a wonderful addendum to all our prayers.

Have you grappled with a situation or a choice and realized that your husband or even a coworker was on a completely different page regarding it? Each person has different goals and perspectives. It's the same with our relationship with God. Hopefully, as we grow in Him, we're embracing God's mind-set more and more.

If we could so humbly approach the throne of God that our thoughts are open to His, we might be surprised to see how our prayers fall into line with His will for our lives. Then we'd be so encouraged that we'd seek His will in all our petitions—families, children, jobs, relationships, marriage, business dealings, sickness, death, life, and so on.

Father God, I don't want any of my prayers to be different than what You know is best for me. May I be humble in petitioning my heart's desires. I truly don't want them if they would not be good for me. I want my prayer to be in Your will and I want my perspective to be Your own. Give me Your heart and perspective. Amen.

Take Action

For the next month add Charles Spurgeon's disclaimer at the end of your prayers. See if it changes the type of requests you make.

Your Reflections

_____

_____

_____

Plan for Success

*I realized that it is good and proper for a man to
eat, drink, and to find satisfaction in his toilsome
labor under the sun during the few days of life God
has given him—for this is his lot (Ecclesiastes 5:18).*

We are familiar with the saying, "Successful people do what unsuccessful people aren't willing to do." If we were willing to pay the price, we might all be CEOs of our own company, be in the Olympics, host our own cooking show, or be the best at whatever we did.

We all have 24 hours or 1440 minutes or 86,400 seconds in a day. To get the most out of life, we need to make wise decisions based on what life means to each of us. None of us plan to fail, but we'll fail every time if we don't plan to succeed. Success doesn't come by luck or accident—it comes because we plan a schedule and schedule a plan.

Of course, our version of success is also likely to be different from that of our friend or neighbor. We are all unique, and God places different passions and purposes on our hearts. While we might not want to run a company, we may want to manage our home and our families with greater ease. We might want to start a community garden. Or maybe our version of success looks like spending more time with our spouse and less time at the office.

Whatever vision of success it is that God has placed on your horizon, it will take effort to achieve it. Organize your day and decisions based on the priorities you know are necessary to move toward that vision. When it comes to making good decisions for the family, you need to be following the plan you and your spouse have for life.

Remember that having no plans for the future will definitely muddy the water in deciding what to do today.

Seek God's paths and the lessons along the way. Don't worry about whether you are successful by the world's standards; only pay attention to whether you are being faithful to the way God is asking you to go. This is success and this is the way of great fulfillment.

Father God, give me the desire to plan for the future. You are a God of order and I certainly want my life to reflect the same. Help me in my planning. I want to live a life of purpose—Your purpose, Lord. Show me the way to live a balanced life—one of moderation and wisdom. Amen.

Take Action

Write down three things that you plan to do today to make your life successful. Don't limit it to just finances.

Your Reflections

———————————————————————————

———————————————————————————

———————————————————————————

Gifts Within a Box

Thanks be to God for his indescribable
gift! (2 Corinthians 9:15).

I have a dear friend who lives in Arizona, and we have been exchanging gifts in the same box for over twenty years. The postage to mail it is more than double the cost of what's inside the carton that is falling apart. The postal clerk wants us to start over with a new box, but we refuse because that's our thing for each other.

It is amazing how excited I get when I receive this ugly, beat-up box with pounds of clear tape holding it together. But when it arrives, I'm thrilled because it has meaning to me.

That's the way it is in our faith. When God sent His Son for us, it was a very simple occasion, but we received so many beautiful gifts inside. It started in a lowly manger but blossomed into much larger gifts:

- *Forgiveness of Our Sins.* "In him we have redemption through his blood, the forgiveness of sin, in accordance with the riches of God's grace" (Ephesians 1:7).

- *The Holy Spirit Teaches Us.* "The Counselor, the Holy Spirit...will teach you all things and will remind you of everything I have said to you" (John 14:26).

- *Eternal Life.* "In My Father's house are many dwelling places; if it were not so, I would have told you; for I go to prepare a place for you" (John 14:2 NASB).

- *The Greatest Love of All.* "As the Father has loved me, so have I loved you. Now remain in my love" (John 15:9).

Yes, God gave us rich gifts when He sent His Son to earth. By His grace and mercy we are able to know His peace. The world wants to buy His grace, but since we are His children, it is free for us. However, it did cost Jesus His life on the cross.

Father God, thank You for the gift of salvation. Your gift gives me life and purpose and eternity. Help me to be a person of praise and thanksgiving. I want to be quick to give You credit for Your sweet grace. And create in me the desire to share the news of this great gift with my friends. May I never worry about presenting things perfectly so that I let the simple, life-changing power of Your gift be the most important thing. Amen.

Take Action

Today, give a friend a gift. It might be as simple as a phone call.

Your Reflections

_____

_____

_____

Perseverance Is Enduring with Patience

Perseverance must finish its work so that you may be mature and complete, not lacking anything (James 1:4).

Perseverance as a Christian is enduring with patience. When we persevere with patience, we exhibit our ability to stay faithful with calmness and without complaint. This can be a challenge, but with practice, it can become your first response to any life test or trial.

"Commitment" and "discipline" are not words "the world" is comfortable with. People living in the twenty-first century want everything to feel good—but perseverance doesn't always feel good. Okay, a lot of times it doesn't feel good. It sometimes demands pain and denial of self. One year our family went to Lake Tahoe to ski. A bunch of us were learning to ski so we took a beginner's class. That should be easy, right? Well, after the first day, we all had sore muscles and wanted to quit. No wonder we want to jump ship when God asks us to ride the waves of a significant life trial!

I will admit that by the end of the week, our muscle pain had subsided and we were able to ski and not fall down as often. But think about how agitated we can get even when we are pursuing something simple (like skiing) that requires even a brief window of committed effort.

Even if we are rather calm by nature, we tend to have the impulse in us to resolve something as soon as possible. Get the hard stuff over and done with! We might be required to deny our own pursuits and dreams as we wait on the Lord and wait for our life to unfold.

Scripture teaches us some very valuable lessons in this area. We are to persevere:

- in prayer (see Ephesians 6:18)
- in obedience (see Revelation 14:12)
- in self-control (see 2 Peter 1:5-7)

Perseverance can be uncomfortable. Yes. But it also can become an act of spiritual discipline that reaps great rewards. Stay in the waiting game. Ask God to help you remain faithful and attentive as you pray, follow His leading, or practice self-control. He never leaves you alone.

God, in life's difficulties, help me to look to You to see what You're trying to teach me. I so want to be a good student in life and to persevere to the end. Let me not be distracted along the way. Amen.

Take Action

Evaluate which of the ways to persevere you struggle with the most right now. Do you struggle to be consistent in your prayer life? Do you tend to want to do things your way rather than wait on God for direction so you can be obedient? Or do you tend to cross the line and push boundaries rather than practice self-control?

Your Reflections

_____

_____

_____

Live the Promised Land Lifestyle

*Be strong and courageous! Do not tremble or
be dismayed, for the LORD your God is with
you wherever you go (Joshua 1:9 NASB).*

Before the Israelites could reach the Promised Land, they had to cross over the Jordan River. Before they could embrace God's promises, they had to trust Him and brave the river. They had to believe that what they were doing was in His will and would lead them to experience His promises fulfilled.

It's easy to read about these examples of faith and courage in the Bible and still not relate them to our own lives. Not many of us are asked to risk our lives and enter the rushing waters to move forward in faith and experience God's promises! But the truth is that you and I do have those moments when we are challenged to cross over to the other side.

Those of us who are believers have had that moment in time where we had to make the decision whether to jump into a situation, a decision, or a choice and aim for the other side of it in faith. We have had the opportunity to say "Yes" or "No" to the claims of God while risking life as we knew it for His promises.

Is there something happening in your life right now that is challenging you? The Jordan River is a picture of what we need to do in our life. Crossing over means we will need to let go of some of our old ways. Sometimes it even means that we need to let go of false beliefs. Facing change can be difficult and saying good-bye to old habits or even past expectations can bring out our stubborn side. There is a part of us that wants to hold on to what we know and we think feels safe.

But God calls us to keep going, to hope for more and to wait on His promises with courage.

In today's verse we are told how to receive the promises that lie beyond the river Jordan. Be strong and courageous. And feel God's presence as you move ahead in faith.

Father God, I know that You have given me so many promises when I accept You and claim all those promises for the life of me and my family. I can wait on You and Your leading because I trust You. Any challenges I face, I know are faced in Your strength. Amen.

Take Action

Pray about your specific "Jordan River" experience. Feel God's presence during your journey. And consider what you need to let go of so you can embrace God's promises.

Your Reflections

_____

_____

_____

Stand Tall in Your Walk

Don't let anyone look down on you because you are young, but set an example for the believers in speech, in life, in love, in faith and in purity (1 Timothy 4:12).

Whether we intend to or not, the way we act, speak, and connect with people provides an example to others. The question is whether it is an example of what *to* do or what *not* to do! While some decisions require longer stretches of time in prayer and discernment, there are actions and ways that we can know, without a doubt, what the right choice is if we want to be a godly example to friends, our family, and to strangers.

Our verse for today provides the wisdom and instruction we need to do just that. And it isn't advice just for the young! If we pay attention to Paul's instruction to Timothy, we will honor and serve God in these areas:

- *Speech.* Control what you say. Concentrate on the positive and stay away from the negative. Build up others. Consider how your words can hurt or encourage. And don't let your self-talk become a way that you undermine your value as God's child.

- *Conduct.* Make it your objective to be a woman of integrity and honesty who respects others in word and deed. Look people in the eye, exhibit good manners, and show compassion.

- *Love.* We are to love God and those around us. Others can discover God's love when they experience a human expression of His grace. Be such an example of that grace and mercy.

- *Faith.* Do you act to please others or God? Those who put faith into action change lives. Consider how you are living out your faith (or not) and what you might do to share with others the good fruit of your relationship with Christ.

- *Purity.* Maintain honor and spiritual wholeness in your life by abstaining from gossip, sexual impurities, negative thoughts, and deceptive behavior. The world truly needs examples of purity.

Our behavior is a great testimony of who God is and our love for Him. If you keep these specific areas of instruction in mind each day, you will be reminded of God's best for you and the way you show Him to others.

Lord, let me examine each of these areas in my life this week. Show me my weakness in each area. Give me the desire to help me make necessary changes in each. Amen.

Take Action

What areas of your life need to be improved on? Do a self-check on each of the thoughts for today.

Your Reflections

_____

_____

_____

Be an Imitator of Jesus

I take pleasure in infirmities, in reproaches, in needs, in persecutions, in distresses, for Christ's sake. For when I am weak, then I am strong (2 Corinthians 12:10 NKJV).

In a world of people entrenched with self-esteem issues, it's easy to become confused about what it means to be humble. How do we experience healthy self-esteem (a term I don't like) as well as real humility? Since the Bible clearly tells us that we're to do nothing out of selfish ambition—we're to consider others better than ourselves—these are issues that we had better sort out. If we consider others better than ourselves, how do we then hold on to a sense of value and strength? We do this by knowing that our weakness, our humility, and our service to others let God's strength shine forth.

Our worth is in and through God's love and grace, not through anything we accomplish or are. Let's go through an exercise to explore the idea further.

First, evaluate your own abilities. Actually write them down. Under each, write at least five strengths and five weaknesses. What are you going to do with your strengths? What plans do you have for turning your weaknesses into strengths?

Second, list three areas where you are willing to serve. Volunteer your services in one of these areas this month. What does service have to do with humility? Well, humility has three elements that are brought out and strengthened when we really give ourselves to serve others:

1) True humility recognizes your need for God,

2) true humility realistically evaluates your capacities, and

3) a truly humble person is always willing to serve.

Serving others is the recipe for humility and good mental, physical, and spiritual health.

> Lord, I am at a point in my life where I want to be more like You. Let me observe how You served others so that I may emulate those ways in my life. Nudge me out of my comfort zone and give me a heart for others that mirrors Your own. I want to experience the faith adventure in ways that bring Your joy to others and bring praise to You. Amen.

Take Action

Volunteer this week to serve someone or an organization that needs help. Consider how to let God's strength infuse your efforts. Keep a humble spirit as God works through your willing heart.

Your Reflections

_____

_____

_____

Why Do I Love God?

Oh, that their hearts would be inclined to
fear me and keep all my commands always, so
that it might go well with them and their
children forever! (Deuteronomy 5:29).

Have you asked yourself lately, "Why do I love God?"

Do you embrace your heavenly Father because of a personal commitment? Because you like the church community and want to be a part of it? Because your parents are people of faith and you felt it was important to follow their lead? On and on we could go...speculating. Give yourself a bit of time to honestly answer the question.

One day members of our small group from church were discussing this very question. We explored the various reasons we had for becoming and being a Christian. One gentleman stated, "All I want from God is a fire insurance policy." In short, he liked the idea of going to heaven more than the idea of facing hell. At least he was honest with himself and with our group. Hopefully, over time, he will grow in his walk with the Lord.

But his comment made me wonder how many people express faith in God because they view it as a safety net rather than a commitment to a relationship with their Creator. I'll be honest—it makes me sad to think that they would shortchange themselves out of a chance to fully know God's love and transforming grace. God is a safe harbor, but He never intended to be our safety net!

Instead of an inner willingness to follow God, it may take the force of difficult circumstances to turn us toward Him. A considerable life trial might be what pushes us into a deeper dependence on

God, and through that we learn to trust Him and know Him. But it would be so much better for you to fall into His open grace now so that the fullness of His love is understood even before there is a difficulty in your path.

The Lord has always longed for His people to obey Him from their hearts. God doesn't want us to obey Him just because we're afraid of a consequence to not obeying or believing. Stand in God's presence and trust Him now with all of your life. This heart choice will lead to life actions that aren't the result of evaluating the pros and cons of belief, but instead are the result of embracing the promises of God now and forever.

> Father God, let my obedience freely flow from my heart of love for You. Search me to see why I do what I do. Let my actions reflect my love. Amen.

Take Action

Evaluate why you love God. Be honest with yourself. You will never grow in the Lord until you can approach Him in an honest fashion.

Your Reflections

_____

_____

_____

Fears Inside of Us

In God I trust; I will not be afraid (Psalm 56:11).

Unfortunately, our culture says that men have to suck it up and put up a front that all is well with them. They might be hurting on the inside, but they mask the pain on the outside.

The story of King Saul represented that same fear. He was a big man, a fighter and warrior. He also had many fears (see 1 Samuel 18:29). He was in a real challenge with David to see who was the best warrior of all. Because Saul could never come to grips with the demons on the inside of him, it eventually caused his death along with the deaths of his three sons, his armor bearer, and all his men.

Read 1 Samuel 31:1-13. Saul's great failure as a king was his disobedience, which eventually disqualified him from holding the office. Had Saul been obedient to God, perhaps his life would have ended in great glory rather than in dark, tragic defeat. Every day we read about or witness the downfall of leaders, prominent athletes, CEOs, celebrities, and even pastors who have succumbed to any number of temptations, fears, and lies. Of course, this can happen to anyone. But when the example of a fallen person is someone who is in the limelight, there is often a lot of effort by others to shed light on what those inner demons are and how that person came to their ruin. People develop a sensational interest in the case, but beneath that there is also a curiosity about how that can happen to people who seem to have it all.

The truth is that somewhere along the way a person who stumbles in such a significant way could not overcome the fears and flaws from within. It may even have been a very short time in their lives that they were willing to step across the line in the sand, but that is all it took.

Rather than find entertainment in these stories or a fascination with what it took to bring someone to their low point, it'd be good for us to turn our attention to ourselves. Are you at all like Saul and resistant to obeying God? Are your temptations and weaknesses causing you a lot of stress and trouble because you resist giving them fully to God?

Friend, I encourage you to put your trust in God today. Give Him *everything*. And do not be afraid.

> Father God, I know that there can be no secrets hidden from You in my life. Let me search myself to see what changes need to be made in my life. Give me the courage to bring to You all of my troubles as my offering. Amen.

Take Action

Evaluate those things that cause you fear and search God's Word for His instruction and comfort.

Your Reflections

_____

_____

_____

Becoming One, Though Different

*"Haven't you read," [Jesus] replied, "that…the two
will become one flesh? So they are no longer two,
but one. Therefore what God has joined together,
let man not separate" (Matthew 19:4-6).*

My Bob and I had many differences when we met. In fact, there were probably a few people who thought we had too many to ever become a unified couple. But when I became a believer, the other differences really didn't matter. What people don't fully realize is that God can make two people one in Christ. Here is a chart of a few of our differences when we met!

Emilie	Bob
Jewish	Baptist
Lived in an apartment	Lived in three-bedroom home
Didn't know Jesus	Believer in Jesus as Savior
Father had passed away	Mother and father alive
Had a working mom	Had a stay-at-home mom
Loved roast beef medium-rare	Loved well-done roast beef
Loved fruits and vegetables steamed	Meat, potatoes, and gravy man
Seventeen years old	Twenty-two years old
Nonathletic	Athletic
Organized	Not organized
Never had an animal	Had dogs, cats, and horses
Born in the city	Born on a farm
Never had a garden	Always had a garden

I would say that God has a great sense of humor. He created us to be different so our lives could reflect the miracle of making two individuals one in marriage. We don't mind being an example of God's miraculous ability!

What miracle has God done in your life? In your marriage?

Lord, thank You for being a God who can bring two unique people together in Your will and through Your love. When our differences get the best of us and we only see them as divisions, remind us that when we keep our eyes on You, we are united in what really matters. Amen.

Take Action

You and your husband take time to list your differences. Note how each of your opposites are really a strength to the weaknesses of your mate. Just because you are different doesn't mean it is bad. Diversity is what makes life so interesting.

Your Reflections

_____

_____

_____

A Time for Everything

*There is a time for everything, and a season for
every activity under heaven (Ecclesiastes 3:1).*

It's hard to find a quiet moment in the day—a few minutes to relax
and pray and to lean into God's presence. Moments to be still with
God don't just accidentally happen. We need to first decide this is a
priority and then we need to commit to making it happen. As God
appoints times and seasons in our lives, we can appoint times to be
still and be with Him.

Just as we explored in the very first devotion, it takes faithfulness on our part to create a new, godly habit. Sometimes adding in
something new to our life requires us to clear space for that addition.
For example, because it's easy to be more outwardly focused than
inwardly focused, it is helpful for you to clear time in your schedule
and clear your mind of your to-do list or the schedules and needs of
your family for that specific time. This allows you to stop striving for
a set amount of time and just be still before the Lord.

Many years ago, I made my quiet time with God a priority. And
to preserve that priority, I made appointments with God and kept
them. I wrote them down in my planner and I made sure to make
room for these chances to get to know God better, to dwell on things
of the Spirit, and to rest in God's presence.

As we get older, it becomes a bit easier to concentrate on the
inward things. I find I sincerely desire to glorify God more with my
life now. Not only do I want to understand His heart more than ever,
I want Him to use me more, and I want to experience His peace and
stillness. You probably want those things for yourself as well.

The door of stillness is waiting for any of us to open, but it won't open by itself. We have to choose to turn the knob and then we have to choose to make time to enter and sit for a while. All of us need to learn to balance the time we spend in quiet and calm with the time we spend in the fray of our everyday existence.

In Ecclesiastes, Solomon ponders the sovereign designs of God and concludes that all the events of life are divinely appointed. So make time today to be still and to seek God's timing and leading for every part of your life.

Father God, I struggle to take a time-out. I not only need quiet time to rejuvenate my body, but I also need times of peace and rest for my soul. Give me the desire to do both. I strive for a balanced life. Amen.

Take Action

Schedule a time today when you can have a "still time" with God—no excuses please.

Your Reflections

_____

_____

_____

Where Are You, God?

Don't hide from me, for I am in deep trouble.
Quick! Come and save me. Come, Lord, and
rescue me (Psalm 69:17-18 TLB).

The psalmist David is like many of us. We pray when we are in deep trouble. We plead with God to quickly answer our prayers. We come to Him when our human efforts have done no good or have even drawn us into deeper trouble. Our problem may have taken years to grow and reach a crucial point, and yet we want God to work everything out right now! Not tomorrow, but now—and hurry up about it. Have you ever lifted up such an emergency prayer?

Here is the good news: God will rescue us—but in His time—not always at the pace we desire. God offers three possible answers: "Yes," "No," "Maybe—later." This means that we may grow a lot in the area of patience and understanding. And let's face it, a lot of us get to that point of emergency because we weren't patient and understanding to begin with. So our learning curve might be a bit sharp initially.

Yes, it takes work, rest, and placing our hope and trust in the Lord.

I certainly appreciate God's loving patience with me over these many years. For instance, I remember being disappointed when a home we loved didn't become ours. For some reason the deal didn't go through. But with that roadblock in our plans, we were freed up to continue our search for that perfect home. The amazing thing about it, the house we finally purchased was better than the previous ones we didn't get. Yes, I was impatient during the process and I wanted to hurry into the decision. But God was responding with a big "Yes" to my prayers to find the right home for us—the right home for us to dedicate to Him and serve Him in and with. In the middle of that house-hunting process, I wasn't fully catching on. I was afraid God was saying "No," but He was merely asking me to wait for His green light.

From that time in my life till now, I have discovered that the more faithful I am in keeping my quiet time with God, the more discerning I am in seeing how God is answering my prayers. I understand Him and His responses to my longings and needs.

Friend, as you spend precious time with God, you will notice that He is placing a strong desire in your soul to come before Him every day; to be in His presence. I want to be known as a person of "being" rather than a woman of "doing." How about you?

> Lord, let me be willing to be on Your timetable rather than mine. I need to take more deep breaths rather than gasping for air because I'm running too fast. Show me how to "be" in Your presence, and give me a new level of patience to wait with hope and faithfulness for Your leading. Amen.

Take Action

Take a moment to look back at a time when you had to wait for a prayer to be answered. Then consider one specific trait that you learned during that waiting time. How might that have been part of God's answer?

Your Reflections

_____

_____

_____

Saying "I Will" to God

*In everything give thanks; for this is God's will for
you in Christ Jesus (1 Thessalonians 5:18 NASB).*

Many believers are continually searching for the "will of God" in their lives. They are crippled by every decision, and continually question if His will permits them to do this or that. Someone once told me, "The best way to know God's will is to say 'I will' to God." I love that.

A long time ago, when Bob took a job in Riverside, California, it seemed like I cried for the first six years we were there. It wasn't that Riverside was a bad place to be, but it wasn't my initial heart's desire. I couldn't picture us being there and building a life. So because it didn't fit my vision, I responded initially with sadness. I think I was grieving too.

Just as a flower can bloom where it is planted, your heart with God's love can blossom in every location and along every leg of your life journey. God often gives us permission or even nudges us to live and work in areas that we would never choose for ourselves.

I learned to give thanks for where Bob and I were. I also discovered how to look for aspects of our life to celebrate. It is hard to be sad or disappointed when your heart is set in praise mode! Have you discovered this too?

Now when we look back, we both realize that God had a plan for our lives. Today we would not be the people we are without living those many years in a city we were unsure about making a home in. God planted us and we bloomed. He will do the same in your life, wherever you are and whatever life season you are in. Hold closely to this truth. Especially when you are tempted to make understanding

"God's will" more difficult than it should be. If we live by faith and do what the Bible clearly tells us to do, we can be sure the Lord will lead us through the difficult decisions when options may not be clear.

Make it a practice to say "I will" to God so you can be sure to live in God's will!

> Father, let my ears, heart, and mind be open to Your leading. Give me clarity in thought when I have to make those big decisions in life. I do want to listen for Your direction and to trust where You lead me. Amen.

Take Action

God expects us to be involved in knowing "God's will" for our lives. He gave us a brain to think and legs to travel.

Your Reflections

_____

_____

_____

Endurance and Encouragement

*Everything that was written in the past was
written to teach us, so that through endurance
and the encouragement of the Scriptures
we might have hope (Romans 15:4).*

Have you ever thought about how blessed we are to have God's Word at our fingertips? It is there for us to delight in and to hold in our hearts and minds. We can have access to its inspired encouragement and hope. Oh, how we need to have these qualities in our Christian experience. It's nice to know what can empower us in our faith walk. And how treasured we can feel when we consider that words written so many years ago are there to teach us, guide us, and connect us to God.

Scripture offers us what we need to know now and later. We can read it and marvel at the new revelations. I am always amazed how I can read a passage for the hundredth time and gain fresh insight. That's one reason why we need to be in God's Word daily. We are always coming across new mysteries and wisdom that we never knew before. Often it is what is going on currently in our life that provides us with a reason, a backdrop to view a specific part of God's Word in a new way.

Get into the habit of daily reading the Bible because you want to, not because someone tells you to. Even though I hope to inspire you to immerse yourself in God's Word, it is self-motivation that will give you momentum in this important part of your relationship with God. And having a personal desire to do this will also help you on days when you feel defeated and have little endurance, encouragement, or hope. On those days, my friend, when you have almost given up or are tempted to skip your time with God, hang in there. Be faithful. God's Word endures and it will bring such wisdom and wonder to your life...and will counter those rough days with great joy.

May you be encouraged by today's verse to renew that spark of your first love for Scripture. Begin anew today. Be lifted up through Christ, even as He was lifted up on the cross for our salvation.

Father God, give me a heart, soul, and mind that is receptive to all that is new that You are teaching me in Your Word. I want to be a woman who is an encourager. Give me a hunger for Your message and purpose for me so that I might live my days with conviction and confidence. Amen.

Take Action

We all need to be excited about life and then share that enthusiasm. Decide who in your life to encourage this week, and then follow through. Discover how God can use your willing spirit to bring cheer or comfort to another.

Your Reflections

_____

_____

_____

The Meaning of Life

*There is nothing better for a man than to
eat and drink and tell himself that his
labor is good (Ecclesiastes 2:24 NASB).*

People in every generation of life tend to rely on themselves and their own abilities. They chase after the things of the world that bring status, prestige, power, and position. King Solomon was a man who had all these things, yet he wisely took the time to think about such pursuits and he discovered that none of them mattered.

In the book of Ecclesiastes he addressed the question every generation asks: "What is the meaning of life?" He firmly concluded that many things in life are truly meaningless; they just don't make any sense or bring satisfaction. He finally arrived at a point in time when he said, "Everything is meaningless without God." Only God brings richness and purpose to life.

As individuals, parents, or even grandparents, we must come to grips with life and ask the same question. Hopefully we come to the same conclusion. One day our child and/or grandchild will approach us and ask us the same question. How will you answer them? Use the wisdom of Ecclesiastes to form your answer. Only a life centered on God has true meaning, purpose, and joy.

Maybe that's why Jesus enjoyed spending time with children. He knew that they didn't have all the answers and that they would seek guidance from Him. As we get older, we tend to come to Jesus with our preconceived notions, our personal rules, or even a mismatched gathering of half-truths we hold onto like they are beliefs.

Let's come to Jesus in childlike faith and with a child's

openness...eager to learn from our Lord. Delighted to be filled by His love. Desiring to take time at His feet with willing minds and hearts.

> Lord, a woman can do nothing better than to eat, drink, and find satisfaction in her work. This too, I see, is from the hand of God, for without Him, who can eat, drink, and find fulfillment? Amen.

Take Action

If you haven't figured out the meaning of life, begin today. Start reading the book of Ecclesiastes in the Old Testament.

Your Reflections

_____

_____

_____

What Is in Your Hands?

The LORD said to him, "What is that in your hand?"
"A staff," he replied (Exodus 4:2).

In Exodus chapters 3 and 4, we read of the encounter between Moses and God. It's a great story of how God uses ordinary people to do extraordinary tasks. With this passage we see where Moses only saw a piece of wood in the staff he held. But God was asking Moses to see what His power could do. To look beyond the obvious and see how God can take a piece of dead wood and turn it into a living form—in this case a snake.

God was telling Moses that what he had in his hand was all he needed if he was going to be the tool God would use to free the slaves of Egypt and lead them to the Promised Land. After 400 years of captivity God was going to free His people and Moses was the man He chose to do this. But first God had to be sure that Moses was able to be obedient to His calling.

Moses, like a lot of us, wasn't confident. God wanted Moses to realize that all he needed was already present in his hand. Nothing more and nothing less were needed with God leading the way and working through him. At first Moses questioned God by making all kinds of excuses to refuse this assignment.

I've done this with God, have you?

When God speaks to us about our dreams in life, it is easy to bring up all the reasons why we can't walk forward in those dreams, that hope. We self-talk ourselves out of this God-dream. "I'm not tall enough." "I don't have enough education." "My family was very dysfunctional." "I'm on the low rung at work." "Others are so much smarter than I."

We must stop telling God why we can't do something and start believing that with God's help we can do anything. We must stand in God's presence and start accepting that His power and strength are our only source for achieving the dreams He places on our heart.

Realize that what we need to accomplish God's plan for our life is already in our hands. Believe it, my friend. Believe it.

Father God, may I realize that You have already given me all I need. I don't want to be blindsided by what I don't have, but to focus on what You have already given me. Help me embrace the dream You have for me and then embrace the tools You are giving me to be obedient each step of the way. Amen.

Take Action

Look at your hands of life. Are they holding what you want them to hold? If not, let go and grab something else.

Your Reflections

_____

_____

_____

Friends Bring Healing

Nevertheless, I will bring health and healing to it; I will heal my people and will let them enjoy abundant peace and security (Jeremiah 33:6).

Over the years, I have found that my friends mean so much to me. I would not be where I am today without the contributions of support, kindness, and unconditional love that friends have given to me—not only personal friends, but couple friends and family friends.

Friendships keep us sane, fill many needs, and remind us of what we love so much about life. I encourage you to think about how you respond when you're around certain people. Do you respect them? Do they encourage you to grow spiritually and relationally? Are they kindred spirits who share your values? If the answers are "Yes," then you probably feel the support is positive for you.

If you answer "No" to any of those questions, it is important to evaluate if the friendship is mutually positive. If it isn't, it can be good to step back to gain perspective. Does this person take away from your joy and faith? Do they compete with you or use words or actions to tear you down? Friendships are to be a healing balm and an extension of God's love.

While you are taking a close inventory of your friendships, also consider how you are offering love and healing to others. In what ways could you be more attentive to their needs, more supportive of their dreams, and more encouraging of their faith walk?

Having good and godly friends is important. Being a good and godly friend is essential. Think about how your friends pray for your health and healing and support you. And reflect on how you can do the same. Friendships are living, growing relationships that need nurturing to keep growing. God will give you the heart to be a good friend and to draw good friends to your life. What a blessing!

> Lord, I appreciate the close friends I have. I look forward to new friends who will be encouraging and supportive. Give me a big heart...one that can hold many friends and their needs so that I may be prayerful, loyal, and loving. Thank You, Lord, for the gift of friends. Amen.

Take Action

Take an inventory to see who your friends are. Would your mother approve? If not, maybe you need to make a few changes.

Your Reflections

_____

_____

_____

Living a Legacy Life

"Come, follow me," Jesus said, "and I will make you fishers of men" (Matthew 4:19).

When Jesus gave His command to His disciples, He was bestowing on them their call to serve. Our verse today illustrates the directness and power of Christ's commands.

We don't have a wimpy God, that's for sure. And His requests are not just for the men and women of the Bible. They are for us today. He continues to call us into His service and lead us into a legacy life of meaning, influence, and love.

- "Go and make disciples of all the nations, baptizing them in the name of the Father and of the Son and of the Holy Spirit" (Matthew 28:19).

- "A new commandment I give to you, that you love one another, even as I have loved you, that you also love one another" (John 13:34 NASB).

Throughout the Gospels are examples of how we live a significant life. You will note that Jesus taught us that if we want a life of significance and legacy we are to:

- Follow Him.

- Learn, study, and teach.

- Enjoy exciting times.

- Persevere through difficult times.

- Obey Jesus's instructions.

- Be blessed by obedience.

In order for us to pursue a life of significance and to leave a legacy for those who follow after us, we must be willing to replace convenience with obedience.

- "But even more blessed are all who hear the Word of God and put it into practice" (Luke 11:28 TLB).
- "If you love Me, you will keep My commandments" (John 14:15 NASB).
- "For it is not those who hear the law who are righteous in God's sight, but it is those who obey the law who will be declared righteous" (Romans 2:13).

Believe God can use your life to do something significant. A willing heart is all that God needs for you to live a purposeful life.

Father God, help me examine my life to see if I'm on the right path to living a life with purpose and meaning. Let me be willing to cast off all those elements that put a curve in the road. Amen.

Take Action

Are you following the right Person? If not, change course.

Your Reflections

_____

_____

_____

Victory over Fear and Doubt

We live by faith, not by sight (2 Corinthians 5:7).

Someone once told me that fear is the opposite of faith. The older I become and the more I observe people, the more I believe that. I find that in my own life, when fear enters into a situation I am letting faith go out the back door. Just like water and oil, they don't mix.

Jesus taught His disciples the power of faith over fear. Here are five examples:

- Matthew 14:25—Jesus walks on the water.
- Mark 6:48—Jesus walked faster than His disciples could row.
- Matthew 14:29—Peter overcame fear to walk on the water.
- Mark 6:51—Jesus got in the boat and immediately the wind stopped.
- John 6:21—Jesus got in the boat and immediately the boat was at land.

Oftentimes we become fearful when we only see our situation rather than trust that God will provide. Peter is a great example of how to deal with—and *not* deal with—difficulties:

- We are to fix our eyes on Jesus. (Hebrews 12:2)
- We are to be obedient to God's commands. (Matthew 14:29)
- Peter lost his focus and became afraid. (Matthew 14:30a)

- Peter let fear take over. (Matthew 14:30b)
- Peter became faithless. (Matthew 14:31)
- Peter was able to walk by faith. (Matthew 14:33)

A problem with fear is that it can grow in leaps and bounds, even while we are standing still. In fact, *especially* when we are standing still. If fears are taking root and blossoming in your life, it is time to do something. Act, walk, pray, and move in God's strength, which will overrule your fears and build up your faith.

Father God, let me trust You by faith rather than what I see. Don't let there be obstacles that keep me from Your future blessings. You are always with me, regardless of what is happening around me. May my eyes remain on You. Amen.

Take Action

Fear is the opposite of faith. Turn your fears into faith this week and for each week onward by fearlessly following God's directions for your life.

Your Reflections

_____

_____

_____

A Faith Inheritance

*For I am mindful of the sincere faith within
you, which first dwelt in your grandmother Lois
and your mother Eunice, and I am sure that
it is in you as well (2 Timothy 1:5 NASB).*

We might put a lot of thought and time into preparing wills and trusts. It is wise to prepare the way financially for those who follow us. But consider how much more important it is that we tend to the belief system we will be passing on to others. It will either be good and positive or it will be bad and negative. Our heirs will reflect what kind of influence we have on their lives. Paul writes a second letter to his friend Timothy and challenges him to remember the influence that his mother and grandmother had on his life. The apostle encourages Timothy to concentrate on the past, present, and future aspects of developing a legacy. Paul wants Timothy—and us—to "fan the flame" of faith for God. We need to embrace the fact that God has not given us a spirit of timidity (cowardice) but one of power, love, and discipline.

The second part of the legacy Paul advocates is to follow the plan God has given us. The apostle warned Timothy that at times he might have to suffer for preaching the gospel. He stressed not to be ashamed, but to believe and be convinced that Jesus is able to guard what was entrusted to Him by God, including the people who choose to believe in Him. That's essential for us to do too.

Another aspect of passing on the legacy of faith to others is to pattern our lives from what we have seen. Paul stressed that we retain the standard of sound words we learn from him. We are to guard, through the Holy Spirit, the treasure, the gospel, that has been entrusted to us.

The last aspect of developing a worthwhile legacy is to pass it on. Paul told Timothy to entrust these truths to "faithful men who will be able to teach others also" (2 Timothy 2:2). Be a mom who cares about the kind of legacy you leave when the Lord calls you home. Teach your children these truths:

- Fan the flame of passion for God.
- Follow God's plan for you.
- Pattern your life from what you learn in God's Word.
- Pass the wisdom of Scriptures on to those around you and to those who will follow.

Loving God, I want to pass on a godly legacy—one that upholds the tenets of the gospel of Jesus Christ. Let me begin today to take life—and You—more seriously than I ever have. Amen.

Take Action

Make sure that you are leaving a legacy that is worthy of praise. We only have one life. Make it count for those who follow after you.

Your Reflections

_____

_____

_____

Living in a War of Worlds

*Be prepared. You're up against far more than you
can handle on your own (Ephesians 6:13 MSG).*

At the breakfast table the other morning Bob and I were going through our morning devotions. When we finished, we watched the morning news on TV. Afterward, I looked at Bob and stated, "I think the world has passed us by."

As we see where we are culturally we truly have witnessed the world pass us by. As a young couple we felt comfortable in our social, economic, spiritual, and political skin. We lived a normal twenty-four-hour-a-day routine. We woke up, fulfilled our daily responsibilities, had dinner together, spent a few hours as a family, and went to bed.

But that isn't the norm anymore. Our days and lives are fractured by many demands, many directions, and many distractions. No wonder we feel scattered and unprepared when we encounter evil and the struggles that rise up when deception comes our way. When we are pulled many directions, it is more difficult for us to be centered in God's will and to be grounded in His wisdom and truth.

Paul, writing to the church of Ephesus, gives a warning: "Be strong in the Lord, and in the strength of His might. Put on the full armor of God that you may be able to stand firm against the schemes of the devil. For our struggle is not against flesh and blood, but against the rulers, against the powers, against the world forces of this darkness, against the spiritual forces of wickedness in the heavenly places" (Ephesians 6:10-12 NASB).

This is as true today as it was in Paul's time. The church—including you and me—needs to be aware of these evil forces in our world. In

Ephesians 6:13, Paul continues the call for us to be strong: "Therefore, take up the full armor of God, so that you will be able to resist in the evil day, and having done everything, to stand firm" (NASB).

Take on the armor of God in your daily living. Spend time in His Word so that it imprints on your heart and mind. It will become your place to stand and your source of strength when you feel scattered or scared in the face of lies or anything that threatens your faithfulness.

Father God, give me discernment to recognize the evil forces whenever they appear. And give me a heart that desires to be prepared for those moments by being in Your Word and Your will. May I be able to stand firm in my faith. Amen.

Take Action

Spend ten minutes a day praying and being still. Let distractions fall away.

Your Reflections

_____

_____

_____

Two Choices of Life

So I say, live by the Spirit, and you will not gratify the desires of the sinful nature (Galatians 5:16).

Life can appear complex, but in reality, we only have two choices. One choice is to reject faith in God, the Son, and the Holy Spirit. The second choice is to believe in God, the Son, and the Holy Spirit. The first leads to distraction and the second leads to eternal life and the blessing of having the Holy Spirit inside of us. (See Acts 1:8.)

In Galatians 5:13-25 Paul very clearly describes the two choices.

Choice one—leads to sexual immorality, impurity, debauchery, idolatry, witchcraft, hatred, discord, jealousy, fits of rage, selfish ambition, dissensions, factions, envy, drunkenness, and orgies.

Paul said if one chooses these things, they will not inherit the kingdom of God.

Choice two—produces the fruit of the Spirit, which is love, joy, peace, forbearance, kindness, goodness, faithfulness, gentleness, and self-control.

Paul tells the church that those who belong to Christ Jesus have crucified the flesh with its passions and desires. If we live by the Spirit, let us keep in step with the Spirit (in other words, do what the Holy Spirit tells us to do).

I think that at any stage of life, it can be difficult to choose those things that feed our spirits over things that feed our earthly desires. Even if we aren't immersed in sinful behavior, we often make choices that cater to our flesh and indulge our emotions and wants rather than seeking those things that nurture our hearts. Without realizing it, we can spend our time investing in things that are not God's best for us.

At times we might think that choice two is not as exciting as choice one, but the end results put you on the "road of success." Listen to the still, quiet voice of the Holy Spirit and tell Satan to get lost. That's why it's so important to be in prayer and to be reading the Bible each day—then you can better discern whose voice you listen to.

Father God, I want to follow choice two and live my life according to Your teachings. Help me to be strong in You. Let me see clearly the road that I am to follow. Bring alongside of me a mentor who will show me how to live. And let my life be an example to others. Amen.

Take Action

Don't waste your life by living out choice one—you know how that story ends. Go directly to choice two.

Your Reflections

_____

_____

_____

Becoming a Doer of God's Word

*For not the hearers of the law are just in
the sight of God, but the doers of the law
will be justified (Romans 2:13 NKJV).*

Suzanna Wesley, a godly woman in early church history, said there are two things you do with the gospel:

- you believe it
- you behave it

Becoming a doer of the Word requires that you put yourself in motion with the power and truth of the gospel. You get up and move forward. How often does a person go to church, become inspired by the worship and message, and then goes home with no change of purpose? When our lives become quite busy and hectic, I think going through the motions becomes far easier than putting our faith in motion.

There are several verses that tell us we must go beyond just being a hearer of God's Word:

- "If you know these things, you are blessed if you do them" (John 13:17 NASB).

- "Therefore, to one who knows the right thing to do, and does not do it, to him it is sin" (James 4:17 NASB).

- "Even more blessed are all who hear the word of God and put it into practice" (Luke 11:28 NLT).

- "So make every effort to apply the benefits of these promises to your life" (2 Peter 1:5 NLT).

- "Prove yourselves doers of the word, and not merely hearers who delude themselves" (James 1:22 NASB).

As we continue our journey to know God and to enjoy Him forever, we will grow in our faith. As we shift from hearing to doing God's Word, we embrace becoming women of character. In Galatians 5:22-23, we can start practicing the nine fruits of the spirit. We are to: love, have joy, be a woman of peace, have patience, show kindness, be a woman of goodness, exhibit faithfulness, be gentle, and show self-control.

You have to first crawl before you can walk.

Lord, lead me to become a woman of character...of *godly* character. I want to grow in my faith and embrace the purpose You have given to me. May the fruit of the spirit be evident in my life. Amen.

Take Action

Choose one biblical truth today and consider how you will believe it and behave it.

Your Reflections

Fruit of the Spirit—Love

These three remain: faith, hope and love. But the
greatest of these is love (1 Corinthians 13:13).

As tiny babies, we look to those around us to give us love. Later in life, we read books and magazines, attend seminars and workshops, and have long conversations with others, attempting to improve our understanding of love.

During crucial years, we spend a lot of time looking for love in all the wrong places. We search and search for that perfect feeling of love and that one and only person called "a soul mate." Despite our best efforts, we still have a hard time defining love. So what is that sought-after feeling? According to Scripture, it's much more than just a fleeting emotion. Instead love is a decision that we consciously make, and it's shown in how we treat other people. When we love someone, we choose to do what is best for them. We are so lucky that as believers we are given God's example of love and its power.

In John 3:16 we read of the ultimate kind of love: "For God so loved the world that he gave his one and only Son, that whoever believes in him shall not perish but have eternal life." Now *that's* love in its purest form. It is sacrificial. It is unselfish. And this love from God is our salvation.

This kind of love (agape) is the highest expression of love. It comes directly from heaven, and when it enters our hearts, we all are truly blessed with its rewards. "There is no fear in love; but perfect love casts out fear" (1 John 4:18 NASB). Do you realize that we can live a life that is without fear and is fully with God's love? That is possible for us because we know and have received God's pure, unconditional, never-ending love.

If you have ever lived in fear of not finding love or the meaning of love, you needn't worry. You only need to receive all the pure love God offers to you freely, in abundance, and forever. Faith isn't about everything turning out right, faith is about being right no matter how things turn out.

> Father God, let me understand this perfect love. Let me be filled and motivated by it so that I put love into daily practice. Let those around me see You by the love I give to them. Give me a heart that expands beyond my limited human capacity so that I encompass many. Amen.

Take Action

Go to a different level of love than what the world sees around them. Exhibit the love of God in your daily walk.

Your Reflections

_____

_____

_____

The Fruit of the Spirit—Joy

A joyful heart is good medicine (Proverbs 17:22 NASB).

Many times we expect the fruit of joy to bring us unlimited happiness and fun times. Yet when we read Scripture, we are encouraged to reflect on what it really means to experience joy and to have a joyful heart and a joy-filled life.

"I have told you this so that my joy may be in you and that your joy may be complete" (John 15:11). Happiness and fun are good in themselves, but they come and go with circumstances. Joy, however, is not tied to our circumstances. It is beyond what we are going through, what we are thinking, or what we have as a daily challenge. While happiness is affected by cause and effect and that is how the world relates to a sense of inspiration, God provides us with an experience far beyond happiness. His joy can be experienced even when times are difficult.

Joy becomes the fruit of our faith and an attitude that we come to know through our relationship with God. His faithfulness brings us joy. His love opens us up to a greater capacity for joy.

This joy from our heavenly Father is a treasure of the heart, a comforting knowledge of God's intimate presence. As we view the events of our life, we can choose to be resentful toward God for letting certain things happen to us or we can choose an attitude and a commitment to joy.

I'm telling you right now, joy is our best choice. We are so blessed by God's goodness. Let cheer pour forth from your heart and soul, even when there is sorrow, change, discomfort, or uncertainty. Even when we don't know what is up ahead, we can be certain that God is in charge of what is up ahead. In that assurance, we find joy. And when we learn to take circumstances and the ups and downs of life in stride and use all situations to bring glory to God, we live out joy.

When we have joy in the Lord, we begin to see life from God's point of view, and we realize that things have never looked so beautiful or felt so upbeat. The joy of the Lord is our strength (Nehemiah 8:10). Be strong in the joy of the Lord, my friend.

God and joy of my life, You know that joy belongs with love, and that our entire being should reflect this great virtue. I thank You for the joy of my salvation. I praise You for always being God and my source of hope no matter what I face. This is my joy. May my life bring You joy, my dear Lord. Amen.

Take Action

Show a deep down joy of the soul, even when you are having a terrible, awful day.

Your Reflections

_____

_____

_____

The Fruit of the Spirit—Peace

The LORD gives strength to his people; the LORD
blesses his people with peace (Psalm 29:11).

Peace is a dream on the global front. We see banners that call for peace. Peace symbols adorn buses, backpacks, and bumper stickers. Peace is pleaded for everywhere and in every language. There are very few people in our world who do not wish for peace on the large horizon and also in their personal spirit.

The good news is that we do not need to search for external remedies for a restless heart or spirit. If trouble brews within us, we can skip the search for a material solution. Our peace comes from God and His blessing. And it is received within our spirit. Our God is mighty and He is also peaceful. We don't have to do the work of trying out different offerings of the world to ease our turmoil because God has done the work. We do have to receive His strength and peace, however.

The world's peace is temporary and comes with strings attached. There is not a lasting effect or transformation that occurs with peace that does not permeate our soul and being. "Peace I leave with you; my peace I give you. I do not give to you as the world gives. Do not let your hearts be troubled and do not be afraid" (John 14:27).

The peace that God gives is built on the awareness that we all need a purpose and a cause for existing. As we mature in our spiritual nature and learn what this life is all about, we come to accept that only our heavenly Father can give us a calmness within ourselves. Once we realize this, we no longer must toss and turn trying to find answers to our struggle. There is assurance and peace when we believe that we have been reconciled with God through Jesus, that our life has meaning, and that we are created in God's image. When we understand these truths, we can move on in life in a very meaningful way. We are at peace with God, and we finally know who we are. We are His.

God, I have longed for peace. Now I embrace the peace that is a by-product of knowing You and Your Son, Jesus. I am glad to be done with confusion and chaos. I feel so free in Your love. Your peace releases me from burdens and inspires me to see beyond the day's troubles to Your promises. Amen.

Take Action

Be a peacemaker today. Step out and give comfort to someone who needs your pat on the shoulder.

Your Reflections

_____

_____

_____

The Fruit of the Spirit—Patience

*Rest in the L*ORD *and wait patiently*
for Him (Psalm 37:7 NASB).

Our culture today is not in the habit of waiting. But having patience requires that we must learn how to wait. While that isn't always fun, it is rewarding to become a person who can wait for God's leading, timing, and answers.

Over the last eighteen years I have had to learn patience while I've spent endless hours in doctors' offices and hospital waiting rooms counting down the minutes until I could receive word from surgeons about the latest news or diagnosis. Bob and I often had to patiently wait to get the results of a test only to find that I had to have another test or exam. I suppose we endured many, many months of "hurry up and wait." That takes its toll on a life. You can begin to feel that progress is out of reach.

While I didn't ever give up my hope and faith in God, I did have times of unrest. The waiting was not easy for me. I am the kind of person who likes to take charge and accomplish things according to my own schedule. Just like anyone else, I had to learn to trust the fruit of the spirit.

Still, I must continually work at being patient, letting God still my soul and show me His plans. I'm not always pleased with what He sends my way. I've often half jokingly told family and friends that I'm going to stop praying for patience because God always sends me such challenges in response!

Somehow, though, the Lord knows exactly what I need to quiet my soul to listen to His voice. My patience has grown with time. Here is a verse to encourage you to embrace patience. "I waited patiently for the LORD; and He inclined to me, and heard my cry" (Psalm 40:1 NASB).

The Lord will hear you in your time of waiting and your time of need.

Father God, You make me a better person as You form my faith and character during times of waiting. You show me that there is no value in wishing away time or circumstances that cause me discomfort. There is more value in using times of waiting and hoping to rest in You and to count my blessings. I realize that important issues often take extended times of waiting. Amen.

Take Action

Okay, you chose the wrong line at the market. Now is the chance to check your patience quotient. Use one delay or incident today to practice your patience!

Your Reflections

_____

_____

_____

The Fruit of the Spirit—Kindness

*Be kind and compassionate to one another, forgiving each
other, just as in Christ God forgave you (Ephesians 4:32).*

Kindness is reflected by speaking and acting with authentic concern
for others, mindful of their needs. It is very much an attitude of the
heart and it is an attitude that develops, matures, and becomes more
and more a part of us when we walk with God and desire to be an
expression of His love to others.

Heartfelt words and helpful deeds will always ease another's day.
That is simple to do, right? But it isn't always second nature when
we get lost in the busyness and details of all we are trying to do and
accomplish. We forget how the simple grace of being kind is an amazing gift to give and to receive.

Kindness does take intention on our part. Each day we can lighten
someone's load and bring them joy by treating them nicely. It's worth
it to make others feel important and to be courteous and generous to
the people we meet, friends or strangers. A bright smile paired with a
genuine compliment convey attention.

If we start each morning considering that our kind actions and
efforts are not only received by the person we extend them to, but are
received by the Lord, it can greatly impact our disposition and generosity of spirit. "One who is gracious to a poor man lends to the Lord,
and He will repay him for his good deed" (Proverbs 19:17 NASB).

Saint Francis of Assisi said it so well: "Lord, make me an instru-
ment of Thy peace; where there is hatred, let me sow love; where there
is injury, pardon; where there is doubt, faith; where there is despair,
hope; where there is darkness, light; where there is sadness, joy."

There are so many ways that we can be God's hands, eyes, ears, and heart to those we encounter. We can consider it a privilege to be His love in the world.

Lord, I come to You this day with great conviction that the kindness we show to others is an accurate measure of how we are living out our Christian life. I want to be a person who others know as a kind person. Amen.

Take Action

Surprise someone today. Be unexpectedly kind to someone.

Your Reflections

_____

_____

_____

The Fruit of the Spirit—Goodness

*Surely goodness and lovingkindness will follow
me all the days of my life, and I will dwell in the
house of the LORD forever (Psalm 23:6 NASB).*

Did you know that the Greek word for "good" appears more than one hundred times in the New Testament? The translations of the word vary to include such meanings as: genuine, honorable, healthy, generous, dependable, and honest. Goodness involves habitual actions which reflect a person's inward disposition.

Long before the present-day teaching of the concept of "excellence" in business, education, or church work, the apostle Paul taught this virtuous concept called "goodness" to the early church. While contemporary society might try to equate goodness with perfection, it really isn't about that at all. It is about having a pure desire to serve, help, and encourage without personal motivation or gain. It is completely selfless. Just as God's goodness flows to us without limit, so can our goodness flow outwardly to others in the same way. Again, perfection isn't the goal...but generosity is!

As maturing Christians, we are to grow into people of goodness. Each day we have the opportunity to show this fruit at work in our lives. The first step is to become aware of those around us who need a touch of goodness. Much as we'd like to, we can't show goodness to the whole world. However, we certainly can touch those with whom we have daily contact—our spouse, our children, our extended family, our neighbors, and our coworkers.

The world is so hungry to have goodness come its way. It takes so little effort to have a positive effect on those you know. Goodness is love in action. It is easy to touch a longing and hungry world that desperately seeks people who give of themselves to enrich the lives of others.

Lord, let me slow down long enough to notice those around me who need a touch of goodness. Help me extend myself, even if out of my comfort zone, so that I offer goodness and kindness to people You bring into my life. Amen.

Take Action

Let someone look inside of you today. What will they find? I hope goodness.

Your Reflections

_____

_____

_____

The Fruit of the Spirit—Faithfulness

A faithful man will be richly blessed (Proverbs 28:20).

In our lives, we are repeatedly challenged to understand what it means to be faithful. We know we're supposed to be dedicated and committed, but when we see wavering of faithfulness in the lives of those around us, how can we still remember what it means to have this virtue?

There are plenty of examples in our culture of how to give up when things get difficult, go for what we want over what is best for others, and evaluate the personal benefit of following through before committing to anything.

In other words, we are taught by example to see whether faithfulness gives us a benefit rather than to pursue faithfulness with complete trust that it *is* the benefit. It is the reward. And it is the joy.

The first thing we must do is look at our actions. When we are exhibiting this fruit we show up on time, do what we say we are going to do, and finish the job. One of our family's favorite mottoes is "Just do what you say you are going to do!" A successful life is based on trust and faith. Throughout the Old Testament we read of God's faithfulness to His people of Israel. No matter how much they complained about their situation, He remained faithful to His promises.

In the New Testament, Jesus reflected the same loyalty to His heavenly Father. Jesus always sought God's will. His faithfulness to the Father took Him all the way to the cross. Even though people today adjust their actions based on our changing interpretations of faithfulness, the absolutes of Scripture make it very clear what it means for a Christian to be faithful. Someday we will stand before

God and He will welcome us into heaven by saying, "Come in! Well done, good and faithful servant."

Father God, I so want those around me to know that I am a faithful follower of You. I want to be dependable, accountable, on time, and keeping my commitments. Thank You, God, for showing me how to be faithful in all that I do. Amen.

Take Action

How faithful are you? What areas do you need to work on? Ask a friend to hold you accountable.

Your Reflections

_____

_____

_____

The Fruit of the Spirit—Gentleness

*Blessed are the gentle, for they shall inherit
the earth (Matthew 5:5 NASB).*

A man saw a blind woman standing on a busy corner waiting for someone to help her cross the intersection. He stepped up to her and asked, "May I go across with you?" That is a definite gentle-man in action. Compassion put into action can be one of the most direct ways to express gentleness. Even listening closely to a person share about their life or needs illuminates this idea of putting compassion into action.

We are a bit disconnected from the concept of gentleness in our culture, although the image of a mother being gentle with her child is still a strong idea that is embraced and encouraged. If we think of this image as an example, we can easily make the leap to thinking about Jesus holding us as His children. There is tenderness and great love in such a thought, isn't there?

The world often equates being gentle with being a coward and an easy pushover! So maybe we steer away from gentleness because it is perceived as the opposite of strength. But we know that is not the case. Gentleness takes uncommon strength. In fact, when I look at the gifts of power and strength, I'm always amazed and more impressed when I see gentleness exhibited along with these qualities of might. They aren't opposites, they are great complements.

A little girl holds a china cup delicately so it won't slip and fall to the floor. A mother animal carries her young tenderly in her mouth. A friend rubs your back when it is stiff and aching. A father shows his young son how to tie his shoes. An older sibling wipes away the tears of little sister who has fallen. Gentleness is a virtue that brings to mind such gestures of sensitivity and care.

As followers of Jesus, our job is to transfer and apply this fruit of the Spirit into Christian action. We will become all that God wants us to become when we reflect a spirit of gentleness in our Christian walk. We also receive this gentleness in the loving arms of our Savior.

Father, it is obvious that You cherish a gentle spirit in Your children. I give You my life so that You can use me to show care to others. Thank You for being my gentle Shepherd. You lead with compassion and speak to my heart with such gentle words of guidance. Amen.

Take Action

Spend a few moments thinking of all the images of gentleness you can. Then consider how you might express gentleness in your attitude and gestures today.

Your Reflections

_____

_____

_____

The Fruit of the Spirit—Self-Control

*Make every effort to add to your faith goodness; and to
goodness, knowledge; and to knowledge, self-control;
and to self-control, perseverance (2 Peter 1:5-6).*

In Romans 7:15-25, the apostle Paul deals with a classic problem
when he struggles to exercise self-control in his life. "For I have the
desire to do what is good, but I cannot carry it out. For what I do is
not the good I want to do; no, the evil I do not want to do—this I
keep on doing" (verses 18-19). Like Paul, we must often work to let
the fruit of self-control grow in our lives and help us to do what is
right. And like Paul, we might become frustrated when we desire to
do what is good and right but it isn't automatic. Many people, including Christians, face such struggles. There isn't anything wrong with
needing self-control. But there is something wrong if we choose to
acquiesce to that temptation or plight rather than giving God control over that area.

When in your life have you struggled with self-control? Or is there
an area of your life right now that presents that tension between trying to do good but failing? Don't let times of weakness cause you to
fall into the darkness of despair. Remember that God's strength is
available to you.

Like an athlete or expert in any field, we should focus upon
improving our skills. Our "field" as Christians is to become more
and more Christlike in our behavior and desires. And like the other
fruit of the spirit, self-control will take effort to cultivate, maybe even
more effort than the others. We don't talk a lot about self-control in

the church or, let's face it, with our friends. But it is an important part of our faith journey and growth.

What few people realize is that self-control leads to freedom. When you give your burdens to God and are no longer weighed down by them, you are free and can face your future and dreams without feeling anchored by struggles. The key to our self-control is always going to be giving God *all* control. Be encouraged and seek out God's leading.

You will be ushered into a satisfying new life of self-control and freedom.

> Lord, we live in a day where people want to be in control, and I certainly want to have control of myself, but only under Your power. Each day help me to remember to give my life to You. May I be reminded that You are the one who gives me control of myself. Amen.

Take Action

Say "No" to good things and save your "Yes" for the best.

Your Reflections

_____

_____

_____

A Genie in the Bottle

I will listen to what God the LORD will say; he
promises peace to his people, his saints—but
let them not return to folly (Psalm 85:8).

How can a little plastic card be so full of good news and at the same time bad news? A credit card is the "genie in the bottle" that presents someone with the possibility of their wants being met. Anything money can buy, right? But of course, that card isn't money. It is debt. And the delight we might feel with an initial purchase is then dashed when the bill comes and when the balance grows.

A simple piece of plastic can give us a pass to the world of make-believe. While it can be so nice to have something today that is beyond your checking account's capacity, you are actually taking away from tomorrow's financial opportunities and freedom.

Why discuss money again in a Bible-oriented devotional? Because God's Word encourages us to address money along with our stewardship. And in today's verse, we are also reminded how we are to avoid folly. God gives us so much and He is faithful in His promises. So we are to be wise and thoughtful in our choices and actions so that we do not go the way of the fool and turn from God's best.

We can't walk in God's best if the monster of debt controls our lives. Pay off the balance at the end of each statement. If you're behind, stop using your card. Never purchase a large item on the same day you have the impulse to buy. Stay within your limit line, and use only one card for all your expenses. Cut up your cards if you can't manage them properly.

Give these four financial secrets a try:

1. Earn little by little.
2. Save little by little.
3. Share your blessings with others.
4. Stay out of debt.

Bottom line, when it comes to money, seek paths to security and freedom, not risk and restriction. You will have the benefit and joy of giving back to the Lord.

Father God, let the use of my blessings honor You. Let my actions be focused on stewardship today and security for tomorrow. Amen.

Take Action

Implement some of these financial principles this week. Be honest about your areas of weakness so you can improve.

Your Reflections

_____

_____

_____

Doing the Right Things

*Whether you eat or drink or whatever you do, do
it all for the glory of God (1 Corinthians 10:31).*

All of us only have twenty-four hours in our day—no more and no less. If we calculated how many days we live in an expected life span and then subtracted the hours we sleep, then the hours we drive to and from work or rushing our kids around town, we will see that over one third of our life is nonproductive. And that's okay! But what we do with the other two thirds is very important. We can waste it on doing unimportant things or we can focus on what's important to us and to God.

If God asked you "What on earth are you doing?" how would you answer Him? In Paul's writings to the church in Corinth, he asked a similar question. He tells us that as followers of Jesus we have been put on this earth to bring glory to God in everything we do. But in order to bring glory to God, we must know what brings glory to God.

Do we show the world that we have love in our lives? Do we show mercy to those who need mercy? Do we give grace to those who have offended us? Do we live a balanced life and have harmony in our homes? All these things and more can bring glory to God.

Many people have the wrong impression about God, Jesus, and the church. They can feel like the church is a club for perfect people or a membership of hypocrites. We know that the church is a place for those who love God, who sin, and who have salvation and grace through the blood of Christ. We aren't perfect. But we are saved and grateful.

But those important truths will be lost on them if they don't first witness the fruit of faith and spiritual obedience in our lives. What messages are we sending? Whether you realize it or not, others really are looking to see what faith is about by observing how you're living your life. What really matters to you? Let how you spend your time and effort reflect the importance of God and faith in your life. When you make God a priority, your faithfulness will bring glory to Him.

Lord, may I live my life in such a way that I glorify You. Help me to use my time and resources in ways that demonstrate that You are my priority. Most of all, I want my heart to never be guarded or divided so that I can give to others with generosity and sincerity that reflects Your goodness. Amen.

Take Action

What areas of your life do you want to make more Christlike? Write them down on a 3 x 5 card and carry them with you as a reminder.

Your Reflections

_____

_____

_____

Work—A Gift from God

*If they obey and serve him, they will spend
the rest of their days in prosperity and their
years in contentment (Job 36:11).*

Where work used to be a blessing it has now become a curse. The younger the generation the more work is perceived as drudgery. Work doesn't have to be viewed this way! It used to be that work was perceived as one of God's blessings. People would do their work "as unto the Lord." Somehow, we seem to have lost that tremendous concept. If we look on work as a penalty or a burden, we'll struggle to drag ourselves out of bed in the morning to go to that job. We will live for the weekend instead of appreciating the gift of our daily tasks.

Women who work at home raising children are not immune from the drudgery-perspective syndrome. It can be even worse for them because they don't even have a weekend off to look forward to if they talk themselves into being unhappy.

But I want to encourage you to consider all that you do as an act of obedience and service in *joy*. I think we'd be a lot happier—and much better workers, mothers, spouses—if we recaptured the idea that our work, our wealth, and our possessions are all gifts from God, and that every action, every deed, and every word is a reflection of our relationship with the Lord.

How we perceive work is how our children will perceive work. If we give off signs of anger or hatred of our work, our children will grow up and hate work. If we are in the right job, our demeanor will give a positive reflection upon work.

As Christians you should be the best worker in your company.

Start your day with a sense of this privileged responsibility and you'll find that those simple mundane tasks will become opportunities to honor God.

> Father God, I hope You see goodness in the way I handle the tasks assigned to me. I thank You for every chance I have to reflect Your truth. The sacrifice and joy of my work is offered up to You today. Remind me that my attitude is also an offering. Amen.

Take Action

Evaluate what signals you are giving off about your attitude toward work. Note the negatives so you can turn them into positives.

Your Reflections

_____

_____

_____

Treasured Time

The whole earth is at rest and quiet; they break
forth into singing (Isaiah 14:7 NKJV).

We aren't always sure what to do with or in our quiet times. In fact, I think we try to find ways to be busy because we aren't comfortable with those precious few moments in our day—stillness, aloneness, quietness. Can you view those moments as great treasures?

Is there a part of you that longs for quiet time with the Lord? I know that with our busy days, this oasis can seem like a luxury rather than a necessity, but it really is our primary way to nourish our soul and our relationship with God. Our quiet time is not a gift we give to God—it's a gift God gives to you and me!

When you do make quiet time a practice in your day-to-day life, you realize what an exceptional gift it is. Simply offer Him your time and yourself. He's the One who will provide the quiet spirit. Get in the habit of saying, "Good morning, Lord," and "Good evening, Lord." Start and end each day with time simply being with God.

Remember to be thankful for all the prayers He has already answered. Use this motto, "Praise before requests!" Be courageous in your asking and confident in His answers. But first, have the privilege of celebrating God's presence. His very faithfulness is a promise and a blessing all wrapped in one.

Sometimes it's hard to accept the gifts we need most. Unwrap the ribbon of grace and the wrappings of peace and receive the gift God has chosen for you today in your time with Him. God's WOW is always better than man's WOW.

Jesus, You give me Your time and attention. I want to give back to You my willingness and eagerness to be with You on a regular basis. Thank You for being there when I call on Your name. The gift of Your presence is life-changing. I praise You today for Your love. Amen.

Take Action

Choose a special chair or nook in your home that can become your regular place for quiet time. Make it inviting with a candle, a place for your tea or coffee cup, and a blanket that adds warmth to early morning times. Read the following prayer by St. Patrick:

Christ with me,
Christ before me,
Christ behind me,
Christ in me,
Christ beneath me,
Christ above me,
Christ on my right,
Christ on my left,
Christ when I lie down,
Christ when I sit down,
Christ when I arise,
Christ in the heart of every man who thinks of me,
Christ in the mouth of everyone who speaks of me,
Christ in every eye that sees me,
Christ in every ear that hears me.

Your Reflections

_____

_____

_____

Be Careful What You Worship

From childhood you have known the sacred
writings which are able to give you the wisdom
that leads to salvation through faith which is
in Christ Jesus (2 Timothy 3:15 NASB).

One of the growing trends among Christ followers is to take a little of this from one faith, a little of that from another belief system, and then mix it with the teachings of Jesus. It seems that so many are forgetting that religion is man's attempt to find God and reach heaven, but Christianity is about developing a personal relationship with God through our adherence to basic biblical principles.

The true believer knows that Jesus Christ is the only way to God. "Salvation is found in no one else, for there is no other name under heaven given to men by which we must be saved" (Acts 4:12). And we believe that the Bible is God's inspired Word, that there is no other inspired source of instruction.

> But as for you, continue in what you have learned and have become convinced of, because you know those from whom you learned it, and how from infancy you have known the holy Scriptures, which are able to make you wise for salvation through faith in Christ Jesus. All Scripture is God-breathed and is useful for teaching, rebuking, correcting and training in righteousness, so that the man of God may be thoroughly equipped for every good work (2 Timothy 3:14-17).

We as Christ followers must have discerning spirits to examine other claims. Our authority is the holy, inspired Scriptures. All beliefs and practices relating to one's spirituality must be based on biblical truth—not on how appealing something may sound.

Take in the God-breathed wonder of God's Word.

> Father God, plant in me a discerning heart so I will know what I believe and will be able to not be taken over by feelings. What a wonderful God You are! You desire relationship and You want me to grow. May I always turn to You and Your Word as I walk the path of life. Amen.

Take Action

Know what your authority is in your walk with God. Don't be tossed about in what you believe about God's Word.

Your Reflections

_____

_____

_____

A Promise Kept

She will give birth to a son; and you are to
give him the name Jesus, because he will save
his people from their sins (Matthew 1:21).

No doubt the Jews of Jesus's time who were living under the rule and control of the Roman Empire had to wonder if God would ever make good on His promise to send a Rescuer who would deliver them and set them free.

God had long ago promised a Deliverer who would set His people free from bondage. For over 400 years the people of Israel had been looking forward to when the promise would be fulfilled. But at the right moment in history, the angel pronounced to Joseph that Mary would give birth to a Son who would save His people from their sins.

Every Christmas, as Christians, we are able to celebrate God keeping His promise not only to His chosen, but also to us who were once known as the Gentiles. And every Easter we also celebrate the continuation of promises fulfilled. My sins and your sins are within the scope of God's promise. We don't have to wait until next year, we can claim His promise today.

"He bore the sin of many, and made intercession for the transgressors" (Isaiah 53:12). How are you living your life as a recipient of God's promises? When you let that truth sink in, consider how you might embrace your faith with refreshed inspiration and conviction.

Do those fulfilled promises influence your life as much as you want them to? Did they influence you a lot more when you first came to know and believe in Jesus? When you arise in the morning, think about how you are blessed to walk in those promises with full assurance that God is faithful.

You are a woman who has received God's promises.

> Lord, thank You for making good on Your promises. May my heart be aware of all the promises You have given me. May my reading of Your Word make me a searcher of Your promises. Amen.

Take Action

Revisit the main verse for today and insert your name. "She will give birth to a son; and you are to give him the name Jesus, because he will save [*your name*] from [her] sins." Rejoice in this promise fulfilled.

Your Reflections

_____

_____

_____

Finding Your Target

I will instruct you and teach you in the
way you should go (Psalm 32:8).

If we don't have a target to aim at, we'll never know if we have a hit or a miss. It is such a simple idea, but sometimes the simple ideas are the easiest ones to overlook. Have you had seasons in your life when you felt like you were wandering without direction? Maybe that is even what is going on right now for you. Such times can bring about a sense of hopelessness or aloneness. But God is right there with you.

Let His will become that target you aim for. If you turn to His Word and your prayer time with faithfulness, that target will be clearer and clearer. As you set your feet and heart toward God's will and hope for your life, you can take action with goals. This is natural for some while others have to be nudged toward that habit. Which category do you fall under? No matter your initial inclination, goal setting doesn't just happen. We all have to take time to think long range if we are going to have an effective plan for aspects of our life.

Make the goals manageable. Ten-year objectives are great, but to stay committed and to keep your path in line with God's will, you'll want to keep smaller goals so that when each new day unfolds, you'll know how to proceed.

We can fill our time with activities—that's easy. But goal setting directs us toward a purpose. If my goal for this summer is to read the Bible, then what book will I read first? If I want to memorize more Scripture, when will I begin this process? If my pursuit is to go back to school, what will I need to get in order to apply for a program?

Our goals become road maps that lead us around the next corner.

You don't want to be so entrenched with goals that you miss the chances God gives you for healthy changes or even new goals. And always keep your eyes on your destination. You will manage your time better, and you will have a sense of accomplishment when you reach a clearly defined goal.

> Jesus, I want to keep my eye on You and set and work toward goals that are pleasing to You. Guide me in my decisions. Help me to seek Your face and Your will always so that my objectives are always those You want for my life. Amen.

Take Action

Spend time in prayer this week as you form a short list of goals. Keep that list on your computer, phone, or a bulletin board. Take baby steps toward these goals.

Your Reflections

_____

_____

_____

Conformity Isn't Utopia

Peace be with you! As the Father has sent
me, I am sending you (John 20:21).

In our community, we have people who believe that we ought to live in a perfect world. They do all they can to block out anything and everything that creates noise or might affect the environment. For example, a group wants to ban the burning of wood in the beach fire rings, another group wants to prevent leaf blowers being used by gardeners and landscapers, while there are even people who want to require permits for lemonade stands! Maybe they aren't seeking perfection as much as they are wanting to have every part of life controlled—and in the way they prefer.

For some people, that kind of controlled environment is a utopia. But it isn't very realistic. And is it a place where there is joy and love? It doesn't sound like it. When we have a certain image that is provided as the only image, it doesn't leave room for the uniqueness of God's children or creativity and compassion that happens when people who are not the same do come together with a shared heart.

Unfortunately many of our churches have a certain image in mind of what a Christian is supposed to look like, be like. We expect everyone to look and act exactly the same way. I'm not talking about a legitimate concern of followers adhering to biblical principles and growing in their faith, I'm talking about the superficial ways in which we might judge one another merely to decide who looks like a Christian. Who fits in with a church. Who dresses and worships in the "right" manner.

I do believe that our churches have come a long way in opening widespread arms to people who do not look like "church people." There seems to be no set pattern of how you should look or dress. I think Jesus looks down with a smile on His face.

Peace be with you and peace be with all who desire to come into the body of Christ!

> Father God, Your Gospels tell us that You associated with dishonest businessmen, prostitutes, and people from despised minority groups. Give me a heart to embrace anyone who wants to spend time with You. We don't have to have perfect churches or perfect people. Amen.

Take Action

Think of one area of life in which you want and push for control. Is it possible that God would rather you relinquish that area to His control?

Your Reflections

_____

_____

_____

A Dream with a Deadline

Wisdom will enter your heart, and knowledge
will be pleasant to your soul (Proverbs 2:10).

We all love to dream. Some of us are more daydreamers than doers, but in God's arena, I really do believe that He wants us to think big—bigger than we have ever thought—and then move forward with faith and faithfulness.

Your goals become the stepping stones toward those dreams. And experiencing the fulfillment of them is a great way to stay motivated in areas of life that matter to you. Proverbs 29:18 says if we have no vision, we perish. We're either moving ahead or falling back—no middle ground. Remember that goal setting must include:

- How much

- A deadline to complete

For example: I would like to eat healthier, move more, and lose ten pounds in the next two months. Goals aren't cast in concrete. They just point you in the right direction.

You might want to make a list of the areas of your life where goals are important: physical, relational, financial, professional, spiritual. You get the idea! Start setting goals and be sure to make them measurable.

As we've explored, it is important to first line up your life with God's will. Seek His guidance through His Word and in your time of prayer and reflection. And then create the lists of goals by category.

I think it is a great exercise to do with the whole family. There might be goals, like saving money each month, which would be best served if the entire family is on board. They might even get excited about making progress together. The fruit of wisdom put into action can be great pleasure and joy.

Another good result of doing this in a way that includes children is that they will discover that there are things worth working toward and even sacrificing for. This kind of daily role modeling can influence them in positive ways. Hopefully they will get so excited that they will want to set their own goals.

God, through faith a dream of eternal life is granted. I ask that You would fill my life with goals that are pleasing to You. Lord may my goals carry out Your dreams for me and my family. Amen.

Take Action

Set three goals today that you can accomplish in thirty days. Write them on a 3 x 5 card. At the end of the month you will be so excited to have them checked off your card.

Your Reflections

What Do I Do with a Teenager?

*My purpose is that they may be encouraged in heart
and united in love, so that they may have the full
riches of complete understanding (Colossians 2:2).*

What happened to that sweet young child who used to live and hang out in your home? They became teenagers, that's what happened! This is the breaking away segment of life for them. They are neither a child nor an adult. These are the years when God is checking out your "unconditional love" theory. And your child is continually checking you out to see if you really love them.

I pray that these simple survival tips for those teen years will offer encouragement as well as guidance as you provide encouragement and guidance to your kid as well.

1. Remember your children are God's children; He loves them unconditionally. They won't always be in this phase. (Thank the Lord.)

2. Don't take everything they say or do personally. This is difficult because they can be hurtful and careless with their words at this age.

3. Keep in mind they also have a foundation of love because you raised them that way. They will get back to that, eventually.

4. Accept them and they will be more likely to accept themselves. Try to keep your sense of humor. Usually your children will not become the adult they are as a teenager. Whew, what a relief.

Having teenagers will definitely improve your prayer life. Believe it or not, a teenager will make you a better person and a better parent. Hug that teenager of yours today and let them know how much you love them. Be an encourager. Catch them doing something good and praise them.

Abba Father, I sincerely want to thank You for my teenager. I will draw my strength from You, and I will never stop showing Your love and acceptance to my family. You have never given up on me, and I will never give up on my child! Amen.

Take Action

Just keep loving them, keep communications open, be involved with their friends, meet them for breakfast or lunch. Make time for your kids at every age. Your effort makes a huge impact on who they become.

Your Reflections

_____

_____

_____

Steps to Understanding the Bible

If you confess with your mouth, "Jesus is Lord," and
believe in your heart that God raised him from
the dead, you will be saved (Romans 10:9-10).

No matter how long you have been a Christian, spending time in God's Word daily is a vital part of growing in faith and understanding. There are always new things that God is wanting to bring to your attention so that you will apply His wisdom to your life. You never "arrive" and reach a point where you know it all. The moment you feel that way, you miss out on the amazing, fresh leadings God is offering and your faith can become stagnant. Don't risk a lackluster faith. Ever.

Over the years I have applied several steps to understanding the Bible. They are:

1. Pray for understanding. (Luke 24:27,32)

2. Read it—Pick a book of the Bible and begin to read it through like any other book. (Isaiah 34:16; Deuteronomy 17:18-20)

3. Believe it—You must believe what you read. (Hebrews 4:2; James 1:5; 2 Timothy 3:16)

4. Mark it—As you're reading the Bible, underline or highlight those verses that are the most meaningful to you. (Proverbs 3:3)

5. Record it—Record the meaningful verses in a notebook, journal, or on index cards that you can carry with you. (Deuteronomy 6:6-9; Colossians 3:16)

6. Obey it—Your goal must be to obey what God tells you; if not the Scriptures won't benefit you. (John 14:23)

7. Use it—As disciples, we must read the Word in order to share it with others in our lives. How are we going to apply it in our daily lives? (Galatians 6:6)

Don't miss out on God's message and heart for you today or tomorrow or the next day. Your relationship with Him is alive and active. Walk in that truth and believe it with every breath you take.

Lord, help me to crave Your Word each day. Let me go slow so I can dwell on each verse word by word. I want to immerse myself in understanding and in Your presence. Thank You for all Your inspiration. Amen.

Take Action

Start using these seven principles to improve your Bible reading today. Record in your journal how this changes your relationship with your Creator.

Your Reflections

_____

_____

_____

Today Is the Day

*You need to persevere so that when you have
done the will of God, you will receive what
he has promised (Hebrews 10:36).*

If you are a procrastinator, the idea of putting any goals, objectives, or ambitions in motion can be very frustrating! I empathize with you. And if you have ever started on a productive path and then dropped the ball, the sting of that failure makes you not want to get in gear again.

Maybe you are someone who needs a push. Or a gentle nudge. While this might not sound like a friendly offer, it really is. I would like to help you move toward the completion of a project. Let's work together. Maybe these hints will help get you started.

- Break down overwhelming tasks into smaller bites.
- Face the tasks you have to do right in the eye—focus. Ignoring them doesn't make them go away.
- Make a commitment to a friend and then ask her to hold you accountable to get started.
- By all means give yourself a deadline. All projects don't have to be completed today.
- If you miss a deadline, don't let that stop your plan to press on.
- Give yourself a reward when you have completed the task. It could be just for you or you might include your family.

Your project may be as simple as reorganizing your desk or cleaning out a closet. It could be a bigger task like reviewing your life insurance policy or remodeling a room. Have the courage to act. Don't be crippled by the "what ifs," the "I'm gonnas," or the "I'll do it tomorrows."

Lord, give me the courage to try again to reach my goals. Remind me to bring my desires and efforts to You as an offering of my faithfulness. I want to walk in Your will. I need to grow in this area and I'm excited about what will unfold. Amen.

Take Action

Be good to yourself when you're taking on a new project. If it doesn't all go as planned, give yourself grace. God does!

Your Reflections

_____

_____

_____

Hurry Up, God!

*The fear of the LORD leads to life: then one rests
content, untouched by trouble (Proverbs 19:23).*

I want God to work everything out—*now*! I keep forgetting that God's clock is different than my watch. Don't we all feel that way at times? Maybe work is not going so well or you have to make a decision that will impact not only you but also your family.

When the pressure is on, it is wise...no, it is necessary to remember who is in charge. God is bigger than our fear and He is to *be* feared. Revered. Respected. Trusted. When you go to God with your immediate and long-term needs, it is never misplaced trust.

This is what I do when I run into a roadblock in my life. I read God's Word. And I trust it. "Those who wait for the LORD will gain new strength" (Isaiah 40:31 NASB). I believe that the waiting, even when it is inconvenient or downright painful, is a way to deepen our trust in the Lord and receive new strength. The truth of the matter is that God will rescue you and me, but in His time and not always at our hurried pace.

In fact, while I am feeling fretful about not receiving help, maybe help is already on the way or within reach. I just have to trust His timing and commitment to me, His child. He hears my prayers as He heard David's outcry. I certainly appreciate God's loving patience with me in the midst of the process.

Our battle cry for the moment should be "I wait upon Your Word for my life, Lord. Gladly I wait for Your good and perfect will." Let this be more than a verse you read and appreciate. Let this become your attitude, your motto, your mission, and your way through any season of waiting and hoping.

Father God, slow me down. You are great and awesome. Thank You for the simple reminders of who You are and what You have done for me and my family. Put a strong desire in my soul to spend time with You today in prayer and study. Let time stand still and let me forget all about my schedule. Give me a heart that is patient so that I am willing to wait for Your goodness to manifest in my life. I believe in that goodness and I praise You for it. Amen.

Take Action

Don't look at your watch or calendar, but step back and look at your situation from His timetable.

Your Reflections

_____

_____

_____

Where Are Your Treasures?

For where your treasure is, there your
heart will be also (Matthew 6:21).

We have to be careful about what we consider to be our treasure because our heart will follow. A long time ago Jesus said that our hearts will be found in the vicinity of our treasures. If we look at that in very practical terms, Jesus is reminding us that what we prioritize and elevate to importance in our life will be where our heart and interest and devotion is.

It is so true. We might not want to believe it, especially if we realize that we have placed great priority in recent years over money or clothes or even holding a grudge against someone. Our "treasure" might actually be something that shouldn't be the focus of our time and energy and choices. I remember we once owned a cherry red 1964 Mercedes. The paint was terrific, the upholstery was like new, the chrome was shiny. It was my Bob's pride and joy and he stored it in the garage every night. One week while Bob and I were away on a speaking trip, our son came home for winter break in college. A few of his buddies were also home and they decided they would go to the mountains to ski. Of course the car they chose to make this trek was Bob's treasure.

They connected a rack on the top, attached their skis, and off they went. After skiing for a couple of days they were journeying down the mountain and the rack vibrated loose and started scraping the paint off the top of the car. They only became aware of this damage when they began to take the skis off back home. Oh my, what would our son tell Dad. His perfect treasure was no longer perfect.

At that revelation, we had to decide where our treasure was in life. In the big scope of life, our car wasn't as important as Bob's relationship was with our son. Often these heirlooms have a testimony of faith, perseverance, and trust in the Lord.

Our timeless treasures symbolize our values, don't they? Love, joy, faith, hope, family. We can have many good timeless treasures. Let's be sure we invest in what truly matters now and for eternity.

Father God, let the treasures of the past remind me of Your love and the true treasure of heaven, which awaits me in my future. Keep me from investing time and wasting resources toward trivial or damaging pursuits. I want my heart to be filled with all that is important to You. Amen.

Take Action

Take a look at your priorities, list them in the order of importance. Rearrange them if need be. This can be an insightful family exercise too!

Your Reflections

_____

_____

_____

We Get Better with Age

*Solid food is for those who are mature, who through
training have the skill to recognize the difference
between right and wrong (Hebrews 5:14 NLT).*

As women, we can really struggle with age and aging. While I do believe much of what we see and hear in the media can reinforce those feelings, I think much of our trouble and perhaps the initial feelings come from within. When we have doubts about who we are and our purpose and forget who we are as God's child (no matter our age) then we focus on the wrong things like temporal achievement, physical appearances, and other parts of life that distract us rather than grow us.

If you feel the world will forget you as you age, remember that God won't. He doesn't want us to remain spiritually immature. Every year of life is a year we can discover more about who God is and who we are in God. Every woman is special. And God loves each of us and our unique heart and soul.

I want to share with you some thoughts on aging. Who wants to think about it? Well, it happens. And there are many blessings that go along with entering a new stage of life. One of those blessings for me personally is that I can pass along to you some wisdom I gained in hindsight.

Many of the thirty- to forty-year-old women I meet are so concerned where they are professionally or financially—they thought they would be farther along than they are. I think many of us believe that we will awaken one year and feel secure and safe forever. But we know that our only solid security is in Christ. And we already have that. Right now!

I encourage you today to trust that life gets richer with each new decade. Each season of life has much to offer including new ways for us to know God and trust Him. You know yourself better. You understand how God has worked in your life, and you can share that with others. And you will take greater pleasure in simple times with friends and family.

I love the quote, "Today is the oldest you've ever been, and the youngest you'll ever be again." Savor every minute and cast your worries on the One who loves you in every season.

Eternal God, thank You for the life I have had and for each day of my future. I am so excited about what is yet to come. I want my faith to grow deeper and my life richer. Amen.

Take Action

Do something silly, like you did when you were young. Be sure laughter is part of it! Celebrate your life in every season and reflect back to God the joy He brings.

Your Reflections

_____

_____

_____

Make Room for God Today

Have faith in the Lord your God and you
will be upheld (2 Chronicles 20:20).

Wouldn't it be great if we knew that everything we set our minds and hearts toward doing would be successful? But there are no guarantees—we won't always succeed in every attempt. But, friend, you will be upheld by God. He will not leave you stranded in the ruins of failures. He will lead you with hope and faith into a future.

Today try to make room for whatever God is calling, nudging, or directing you to do. This isn't just something to say to encourage you. It really matters. Believe in those leadings from God and trust that He will be with you for each step required.

When we do take a leap of faith *with* faith, we will discover the joy of trusting God. Most of us need encouragement to take action on something our heart has been nudged to do. So what is it that God is leading you to do? To believe about your future? If you aren't sure, consider what it is that fills your mind as a possibility each time you have a spare moment. What comes into your thoughts and prayers? If you are like me, there is that glimpse of a great hope, and then the inspiration and the moment are gone and you think, "Someday I will have the time to do it and do it right...but not now."

Time goes quickly. Don't put off God's nudges.

But do you realize that success is not really our responsibility? We're just called to do what God asks: share with others about Him, help those in need, and live a life of integrity. And we're to leave the outcome to Him. We may never know the results of our caring deeds. Or we may have the joy of seeing what our "seeds" have done. Either way our job is to be faithful and obedient and that includes taking steps toward the dream God places on our heart. Our God will do the rest.

Pretty simple, wouldn't you say?

God, I want Your view of success in everything I do. May I never hold back out of fear of failure. Please help me see that You work miracles through the frailties of Your children and when I try and good things unfold, You are glorified. Amen.

Take Action

Try to make room for whatever God is calling, nudging, or directing you to do. What call have you ignored for much of your life? Move forward in it with a small step today.

Your Reflections

_____

_____

_____

You Are More Valuable
than a Sparrow

Don't be afraid; you are worth more
than many sparrows (Luke 12:7).

We live in a world that has become confused by how valuable the human being is. Many consider us equal to the birds, the dogs, the cats, and the horses—and no more. But God has placed great value on us, His human creation. He cares deeply about us in our times of need.

In 1905 Civilla D. Martin wrote a great hymn called "His Eye Is on the Sparrow." This hymn and its words have been so inspiring to people who have been sick and are concerned about their recovery, and for people who have questioned whether God notices their need. The song and the sentiment taken from Scripture have been such an encouragement to many and remind us that if God watches over the little sparrow, He will surely watch over us. Reflect on these two verses now and take in God's love, attention, and care.

> Look at the birds of the air; they do not sow or reap or store away in barns, and yet your heavenly Father feeds them. Are you not much more valuable than they? (Matthew 6:26).

> Are not two sparrows sold for a penny? Yet not one of them will fall to the ground apart from the will of your Father. And even the very hairs of your head are all numbered. So don't be afraid; you are worth more than many sparrows (Matthew 10:29-31).

Recently, I had a dear friend of more than forty-five years come down with a very serious form of cancer. During his illness he claimed this line in this great hymn, "His eye is on the sparrow and I know He watches me." Even though my friend was not able to be earthly healed, he was certainly given encouragement to know that God is able to take care of all of us.

God reminds us again and again in His Word and in the way He loves us that He cares for us so very much and in every way that matters.

Father God, You are our Creator and You have planned for our everyday needs. I thank You just for today. May I avoid looking forward or backward and try to keep looking upward. Amen.

Take Action

Look around you at what God has provided. Thank God for His provision and list them one by one to encourage your heart and to praise God for His many blessings.

Your Reflections

_____

_____

_____

To Remember or to Forget

This is my body given for you; do this in
remembrance of me (Luke 22:19).

I love family reunions because we always are remembering things from our past. Our story has more meaning when we remember what we have been through and how God has been present with us along the way. Remembering is important. Sometimes we have spiritual amnesia. The Jewish nation was always being told that they forgot the laws of their God. For example:

- "You deserted the Rock, who fathered you; you forgot the God who gave you birth" (Deuteronomy 32:18).

- "When I fed them, they were satisfied; when they were satisfied, they became proud; then they forgot me" (Hosea 13:6).

Let us not become women who forget what God has done. If we are in God's Word we are reminded of His faithfulness, His strength, and His desire for relationship. This will also bring to mind what we should be doing daily so that we don't forget God in the busyness of our lives. I feel closest to God when I look back at the promises God has given us. In God's Word we are told that He remembers His promises. For example:

- "He remembers his covenant forever" (Psalm 111:5).

- "He has remembered his love and his faithfulness to the house of Israel" (Psalm 98:3).

- "I, even I, am he who blots out your transgressions, for my sake, and remembers your sins no more" (Isaiah 43:25).

The greatest remembrance is what Jesus did for us on the cross—each time we share the Lord's Supper. On the front of communion tables in many churches these words are engraved: "This do in remembrance of Me."

When you participate in the Lord's Supper...and when you begin a new day or cherish a memory of God's faithfulness...do all such things in remembrance of Jesus.

Father God, let me discern what needs to be remembered and what needs to be forgotten. I thank You for forgiving me and for no longer remembering my old self. I walk in that newness every day with gratitude. Amen.

Take Action

On a piece of paper write what you want to forget and what you want to remember. Share this list with a friend.

Your Reflections

_____

_____

_____

Let the Legacy Live On

*In everything set them an example by
doing what is good (Titus 2:7).*

Listen to your words. Watch your actions. Are you consistent with what you say you believe? That is a tough one to master. But it is especially important if you are a parent. Have you ever had your unkind words or expressions come back to you in a miniature reenactment through your child? Oh, what a sinking feeling. And if it happened, there's a good chance it happened in front of others when you could be doubly horrified to see your less than shining moment reflected back to you!

But of course, being consistent in behavior, attitude, and discipline is not just important because you have children. It is important because it is the right thing to do. And consistent, godly behavior is important not only because it might get reflected back to us by our child but because we reflect our heavenly Father.

If we tout the value of calmness and patience, do we respond with patience when standing in a slow line at the market? Where does our conversation go when there's a slowdown on the highway? Do we help people out even when it's not convenient?

We are continually setting some kind of example whether we know it or not. Even when you are in a hurry, take a moment to ask God for a clear mind and eyes that will see where there is a need that you can meet. It takes very little to improve another person's day and lift their spirits. Check in with your neighbor just to say hi. Write a thank-you note to a friend. Send a note and a bit of spending money to a college student facing finals. Greet strangers and coworkers with a genuine smile. Say thank you and mean it.

Let your life be a simple example to all those around you. Do not disappoint God. Make Him proud of His child.

> Father God, I need Your guidance to be a role model for my children and grandchildren. Help me to always be an example of a godly woman. I want to practice what I preach. And I want to live out what I believe. Amen.

Take Action

Do something today that will make your children fondly remember your example, long after you are gone.

Your Reflections

_____

_____

_____

God Loves You

*May the God of hope fill you with all joy and peace
as you trust in him, so that you may overflow with
hope by the power of the Holy Spirit (Romans 15:13).*

When life becomes difficult or when daily stresses get to you, it could be that you are living by your own power and theology. The gospel according to you. And believe me—that is not a good direction. When we draw from our own well, the resources run dry. We lose momentum, motivation, and meaning. However, when we draw from the endless well of God, we gain all those.

Truth is, you are probably much harder on yourself and more critical of who you are than God would ever be. Believe what God believes about you! Here are some simple thoughts to take with you today:

- Because God loves you, He is slow to lose patience with you.

- Because God loves you, He doesn't treat you as an object to be manipulated.

- Because God loves you, He is for you.

- Because God loves you, He keeps working patiently with you—even when you feel like giving up.

- Because God loves you, He never says there's no hope for you. He patiently works with you, loves you, and offers you good choices to make in life.

- Because God loves you, He was willing to give His one

and only Son to die on the cross for your sins yesterday, today, and tomorrow.

Do you feel the love? Can you see yourself in this light and your life in a new light? When you are feeling unsure about your worth, come back to this list and savor these reminders. Live like the loved daughter of the King that you are.

God, I want to wake up each morning and embrace the thought that You love me. I want to believe it wholly. I want to believe what You believe about me and my life. I want to come to the infinite well of Your love for my sense of worth. Amen.

Take Action

Spend more time in God's Word to create your own list about your identity and value in Christ. Keep that list with you!

Your Reflections

_____

_____

_____

We Grow Through Our Problems

Consider it pure joy, my brothers, whenever you face trials of many kinds, because you know that the testing of your faith develops perseverance (James 1:2-3).

Consider our trials as joys? That's a bit difficult for a lot of us. In fact, I'm one of those people who wakes up each morning and starts thinking about the problems that might come my way so that I can try to eliminate them in advance. And if I can't think of a solution, I try to think of a detour. So I guess my general opinion has been that no good can come from having problems.

Do you think that way too? Well, I hate to admit it, but both of us need to think again.

The Bible says problems strengthen our Christian walk. So be glad—yes, glad—that you have them. Here's my prayer as I pursue a heart that is thankful for obstacles: "God, thanks for loving me. I see what You are doing when You give me a new problem. But could You start out slowly? (I am a slow learner.) I really don't want to become a spiritual giant too quickly!"

- Difficulties do seem to make us humbler—because we realize we can't do this life alone and we need God's help.

- Pitfalls make us more appreciative of blessings—because we understand how often we do walk a smooth path.

- Struggles make us strong—because we gather the strength of God's Word, His promises, and His purpose so we can move through the problem to the other side.

- Questions and concerns make us wise—because we seek God's answers and insight.

A world without problems would be a world without solutions. If you reflect on your faith journey, think how many times your connection and deeper understanding of God involved a solution to a problem or an answer to a question. Problems help us see God for who He is...Healer, Creator, and omnipotent director of our lives.

Lord, You know everything there is to know about the world, and about me and my problems. You pay attention to my every question and struggle. Thank You for caring about me. Amen.

Take Action

Be ready to handle your future problems in a godly way. You will certainly have a new problem soon. Be ready.

Your Reflections

A Life of Good Decisions

*The fear of the LORD is the beginning of knowledge, but
fools despise wisdom and discipline (Proverbs 1:7).*

The book of Proverbs gives instruction on living life in a sensible way. It is about choosing wisely. And the fear of the Lord is the first step forward in knowledge and toward wisdom. Those who read and practice the principles of Proverbs, who listen to wise instruction, will prosper in the present as well as in the future.

I have a tendency to try to put something together without first reading the instructions. However, the older I get, the more I realize how futile this is. I now find myself going to the instructions in an effort to do it right the first time. Whether I'm baking or piecing together a toy for a child, I know that there is value in going point-by-point and step-by-step. It makes the creation process so much easier and far less stressful. And wouldn't you know it...things usually turn out right the first time.

The same is true about piecing together our lives. Shaping our days and creating a life is not something we should be winging or doing with bits of information and driven mostly by stubbornness. It becomes the lazy and trouble-filled way through life when we ignore the resource we are given: godly principles.

Instead of floundering and trying to do things on your own, go to the Instructor's Manual first before trying to unlock all of life's mysteries. In several passages of the New Testament the fear of the Lord is said to be man's proper acknowledgment of who He is (see Luke 12:4-5; Ephesians 5:21). God is always present, and wisdom begins when we acknowledge this fact.

The knowledge that Solomon's wise sayings in the book of Proverbs offer us goes beyond accomplishments. His advice centers on moral responsibility—how to make wise decisions and how to conduct ourselves in various situations in everyday life. Solomon challenges us to continually seek God's wisdom in the decisions we make each day.

Father God, You have given me a brain, and I want good information to put in it. Give me proper wisdom, which will give me a basis to make good daily decisions. I want to have a patient heart that will wait for Your leading even when I want to forge ahead with my own way. The wisdom that comes from You is worth the wait! Amen.

Take Action

Make sure you have a good understanding of what you believe so you will know how to make a good decision.

Your Reflections

Listen to God's Commands

*Do not enter the path of the wicked, and do not walk
in the way of evil. Avoid it, do not travel on it; turn
away from it and pass on (Proverbs 4:14-15 NKJV).*

Why is it that when we see a sign that says "Wet paint—do not touch" we automatically stick out our finger to see if it is really wet? As human beings we want to do the opposite of what others tell us not to do. When a sign says "Do not," we want to test the command.

We live near the ocean and there are high bluffs along our strip of beach. Every year, it seems, several swimmers die trying to descend those bluffs to get to the beach, even though there are steel cables limiting access to the danger areas. In all cases, the would-be swimmer has to cross by a sign that says "No Trespassing—Danger!"

One of the most difficult things to learn in life is to be obedient to authority. Today's reading gives three warnings:

1. Do not walk toward evil.

2. Avoid it.

3. Turn away and pass it.

The writer of Proverbs is almost shouting into a megaphone to warn people to stay away from evil. But it takes that decibel level for many of us to actually pay attention to the message. Temptations are, well, tempting. And we often want to test the boundaries and see whether something truly is bad, risky, or even evil.

When we bypass the signs and stop believing in God's instruction—we do so because we think we can handle it ourselves. When do we call on God? After we've already made a mess of things by ignoring the information. This turns even the most stubborn and self-sufficient person into a praying believer!

Let's be the smart ones who read the signs and pay attention to the wisdom and perspective given to us by our Lord so that we avoid evil and embrace a righteous path.

> Father God, let me believe Your signs along the way. Let me trust You when You say don't walk there, avoid it, and turn away. Amen.

Take Action

Take time to think through signs you've avoided or are avoiding in your life. What are you going to do about those now?

Your Reflections

_____

_____

_____

Faith Is a Gift

Now faith is the assurance of things hoped for, the
conviction of things not seen (Hebrews 11:1 NASB).

Do you have trouble believing in something you haven't seen? The disciple Thomas did. He couldn't bring himself to believe in Jesus's resurrection until he actually saw and touched Jesus.

Jesus told Thomas, "Because you have seen me, you have believed; blessed are those who have not seen and yet have believed" (John 20:29). I don't believe Jesus was scolding Thomas when He said these words. He was just saying that Thomas would be a lot happier—that's what "blessed" means—if he could learn to take some things on faith!

I think that's true for many of us. We have faith, and yet we keep asking for proof or more clarification. God doesn't reprimand us because of this. He lovingly reveals Himself time after time. However, we are missing out on the abundance of a life lived out in absolute faith when we question more than we rest in God's peace!

What is so incredible is that every day I take it on faith that my car will start, my TV will turn on, my Internet server will function. These are pretty miraculous creations and they work—at least most of the time. So if I can manage to believe in these man-made miracles, why should I have trouble believing in God and His divine miracles? Even though I haven't physically seen Him, I have felt His presence. I have seen His works. As a result, I no longer waste my energy fussing over whether God is real. I choose to enjoy the blessing of belief.

If you are having a doubting Thomas kind of day or year...reach out and seek Jesus through prayer and Scripture. You will experience

Him. God is not disappointed that you need this reassurance; He just wants you to live a blessed life.

> God, I'm so thankful that the world has not blinded my vision of You and Your glory. I know You are there even though I can't see You. Your presence gives me assurance and peace. I want to savor the blessing of belief. Amen.

Take Action

In what area of your life do you lack faith? Give all your life to God's care, including this area.

Your Reflections

_____

_____

_____

Know Your Position in Christ

To all who receive him, to those who believed in his name,
he gave the right to become children of God (John 1:12).

Who am I in Christ? This is a basic but vital question for us to ask. In reality there are two audiences that answer this question: first, others; second, God.

Man's opinion is short-lived and will soon fade away, but God's thoughts are eternal and everlasting. Nothing is more freeing than agreeing with God about how He sees us. That's why it is so important to be in a daily study of God's Word. When we do, we will know:

- who God is
- who we are in Him
- what we have in Him
- what we can do through Him

Day by day we are to live out who we are as new creations in Christ Jesus. And the list of what that entails is very amazing. Delight in knowing that you are:

- able to do all things (Philippians 4:13)
- filled with joy (John 17:13)
- known (2 Timothy 2:19)
- made by Him (Psalm 100:3)
- an overcomer (1 John 5:4-5)
- a partaker of grace (Philippians 1:7)

- valued (Matthew 6:26)
- walking in new life (Romans 6:4)

I will keep reinforcing how treasured you are and what a wonder you are in Christ, because this identity is your foundation for everything in life.

Father God, no matter what I think of myself, Your Word tells me I am valued and loved. As I look in the mirror may I see the face of a woman who is known and cherished by God. Thank You for loving me so much. Amen.

Take Action

Each day go through one of the verses above and take to heart the value you have in Christ. God likes to take our imperfections and turn them into His perfection.

Your Reflections

_____

_____

_____

We All Need a Spiritual Heart Transplant

I will give you a new heart and put a
new spirit in you (Ezekiel 36:26).

As we meet with God regularly, we realize that our heart, on its own, cannot do what is necessary to make us a godly person. In fact, none of us can make that transformation happen under our own power, and fortunately, we don't have to. God offers us a heart transplant, one even more remarkable than a medical transplant of a physical heart.

Hopefully, none of us will ever need a new physical heart, but each of us does need a new spiritual heart. Why? Because we are all born with a sinful nature.

- King David said, "Behold, I was brought forth in iniquity, and in sin my mother conceived me" (Psalm 51:5 NASB).

- The prophet Jeremiah writes, "The heart is deceitful above all things and beyond cure" (Jeremiah 17:9).

- Jesus taught, "Out of the heart come evil thoughts, murder, adultery, sexual immorality, theft, false testimony, slander" (Matthew 15:19).

- Paul wrestles with his sin nature: "For the good that I want, I do not do, but I practice the very evil that I do not want. But if I am doing the very thing I do not want, I am no longer the one doing it, but sin which dwells in me" (Romans 7:19-20 NASB).

- The apostle John is very direct in his statement about sin: "If we say that we have no sin, we are deceiving ourselves and the truth is not in us" (1 John 1:8 NASB).

So what are we to do? Not even the most skilled physician can cure a sinful heart or give us a new and pure heart. But God can. He offers this transformation to us free of charge, but it cost Him greatly—He gave us His only Son for our salvation. All we have to do is accept it. Once you have a changed heart, you have a changed life. You can love the unlovable, be kind to the unkind, and forgive the unforgivable. All this because you have a new heart—a God heart.

Father God, give me that newness of spirit that refreshes like the spring water that flows through the valley. Change my heart and my mind to be in line with Your will and Your hope. Amen.

Take Action

Spend time this week thinking about what it means to have a new heart. Discover ways your new heart helps you to love, care, and forgive more than your old one.

Your Reflections

_____

_____

_____

Live for Today

*May the God of hope fill you with all joy and peace
as you trust in him, so that you may overflow with
hope by the power of the Holy Spirit (Romans 15:13).*

It seems like we spend so much time thinking of what we didn't do yesterday and worrying about tomorrow that we forget the only day that counts—today.

As I've observed children over the years, one thing stands out very vividly—their ability to live and enjoy the moment. They can take the "now" and make it a gift. I'm trying to forget about what happened yesterday and what might happen tomorrow and just experience the fullness of today.

In order to capture the present, we need to give less attention to worries, mistakes, possible wrongs, general concerns, things to get done, the past, the future, and the undone. Often our anxieties are about situations we have no control over. Why spend all that negative energy on something that probably will never occur? One of our family's bits of wisdom for life is "85 percent of the things we worry about never come true." In truth, the percentage is probably much higher. When you view your concern from this angle, doesn't it seem silly to worry so much?

Living without regrets for the past or fears about the future ushers in a new freedom to taste the joys of each day. When you do this, all your focus is on the now. You can smile, laugh, pray, think, and enjoy what each moment brings.

We are to stop and smell the roses, listen to the train whistle, pause to imagine shapes in the puffy clouds in the sky, hear the rain pitter patter, or watch the snow fall. If this doesn't sound very much like an exercise in faith, consider how finding pleasure in these things draws you into the moment and how times of awe and joy connect us to our Creator's joy. When we begin to see and experience every minute, we will also begin to see the grandeur of God and His vastness.

Father God, pull me back from my frets of yesterday and my worries of tomorrow so that I can savor today. I don't want to miss out on anything You are showing me in this present moment. And I don't want to waste my days on imagined concerns when You place real opportunities for faith in my path. Amen.

Take Action

Practice saying and living this thought: *Today, I will only think about today.* How difficult is that for you? Try this every morning for a week and see if you are more present to God as the week goes on.

Your Reflections

_____

_____

_____

Learn to Be Still

On the seventh day God rested from
all his work (Hebrews 4:4).

From the beginning of creation it was intended for man to have the seventh day to rest. God had no intention or desire for us to become addicted to work. Our American culture at one time stopped everything to set aside Sunday as a day of rest (called the blue laws). Little by little over the years we compromised that principle and today our commercial enterprises have their busiest sales day on Sundays. The markets are packed and we have to wiggle our way through the malls.

The urgency of doing, doing, doing feels like it came from nowhere. Nevertheless, it has become our way of life. But that isn't God's intention for us. Why is rest so important? Let's look at a couple reasons.

1. *God commands it.* His second command in Exodus 20:8 states, "Remember the Sabbath day by keeping it holy." The Sabbath served as a holy day and a day of rest for both man and animals, commemorating God's rest after the work of creation. In Acts 20:7 Paul and the church observed the Sabbath on the first day of the week (Sunday).

2. *It was part of God's lifestyle.* "For in six days the LORD made the heavens and the earth, the sea, and all that is in them, but he rested on the seventh day. Therefore the LORD blessed the Sabbath day and made it holy" (Exodus 20:11). This is a day set aside to rest, spend time with the family, read good material, reflect, and even find time to catch up on sleep.

3. *We are to reflect on the past and where we've come from.* We

were not always believers. Each of us has our own story of salvation. We are to reflect back as an individual as well as a group of people. God always wants us to remember where we have come from. In Deuteronomy 5:15 we read, "Remember that you were slaves in Egypt and the LORD your God brought you out of there with a mighty hand and an outstretched arm."

God releases us from our burdens. When we are enslaved to the world, it is God and God alone who desires to lead us to our place of freedom.

Father God, let me trust Your desire for me to take one day each week and rest. Let me value Your examples in Scripture that tell me it is good for my soul. When I get anxious about things that are left undone or that creep into my thoughts during times of rest, guide me back to Your peace. Shape my spirit to be a patient, attentive one. Amen.

Take Action

Establish a plan that will purposely let you set apart twenty-four hours to celebrate your Sabbath. Count your blessings that will follow.

Your Reflections

_____

_____

_____

The Four Soils

As he was sowing, some seed fell beside the road, and
the birds came and ate it up (Mark 4:4 NASB).

In the four books of the gospel, Jesus used parables to teach His disciples and fellow believers. A parable is a short story that illustrates a lesson, a teaching, a truth. Parables were told by Christ to make the truth more engaging and clear to those who were willing to hear and to make the truth obscure to those who lacked spiritual concern.

In this particular parable Jesus is trying to teach that seeds (the Scripture or Word) will have different effects depending upon the soil (the heart) in which they land.

In all cases, it is the quality of the soil that makes the difference between something growing or not. Some people have ears to hear and some don't. I'm sure that in each case the people wanted to hear, but for various reasons the seeds (Word) never stuck. That's the way it is in our lives. Some hear or read Scripture but it has no impact.

Mark 4:15-20 is a verbal picture of what happens when the seeds land on the four different soils:

1. Some people are like seeds sown along a path. They hear the Word, but Satan comes and takes away the Word that was sown in them (verse 15).

2. Some people are like seeds that are tossed on a rocky place, which represents the person who receives the Word joyfully, but has no firm root; then when persecution arises because of the Word, they fall away (verses 16,17).

3. Still other people are like seeds that are sown among the

thorns; these are ones who have heard the Word but the worries of the world and the deceitfulness of riches and the desires for other things enter in and choke the Word and they become unfruitful (verses 18,19).

4. And then there are the people who are like seed sown on good soil; they hear the Word, accept it, and bear fruit thirty, sixty, or even a hundredfold (verse 20).

Which soil are you? You may know friends and family members of each example. May the truths and promises of God's Word abide in you forever.

Father God, I have found myself at different stages of faith. Thank You for sticking with me and letting me see You working in other people's lives through me. Create in me a heart and soul that is receptive to Your Word so that it takes root and grows in my life. Amen.

Take Action

Examine your heart and life today to figure out which soil truly represents you and your ability to accept God's Word and let it take root in your life. Be patient with God. Be patient with yourself. Consider how to cultivate the richest soil to receive and nurture and foster God's truths in your life.

Your Reflections

_____

_____

_____

Be the One to Say "Thank You"

He fell to the ground at Jesus' feet, thanking him
for what he had done (Luke 17:16 NLT).

In this passage of Scripture found in Luke 17:11-19, we read the story of the ten lepers who were healed by Jesus.

> As Jesus continued on toward Jerusalem, he reached the border between Galilee and Samaria. As he entered a village there, ten lepers stood at a distance, crying out, "Jesus, Master, have mercy on us!" He looked at them and said, "Go show yourselves to the priests." And as they went, they were cleansed of their leprosy. One of them, when he saw that he was healed, came back to Jesus, shouting, "Praise God!" He fell to the ground at Jesus' feet, thanking him for what he had done. This man was a Samaritan. Jesus asked, "Didn't I heal ten men? Where are the other nine? Has no one returned to give glory to God except this foreigner?" And Jesus said to the man, "Stand up and go. Your faith has healed you."

To be a leper meant you were an outsider—no one wanted to be around you. You were isolated from the rest of the community—in many areas lepers were sent to a lonely island or region where they lived apart from others. But Jesus had compassion on these ten men who had this dreaded disease. He not only healed the ten men, He also commanded that they go and show themselves to the priests. In that time and culture, the priests were the ones to examine them, declare them healed, and give them the okay to be able to blend back into the community. People were in awe of Jesus's response.

What is fascinating about this story is that the only leper who came to thank Jesus was an outcast of the Jews—a Samaritan. This makes the moment all the more powerful. That precious thank-you came from someone who was an outcast on many levels. But he broke through those boundaries to thank the Lord just as Jesus broke through the boundaries to heal him.

What about you? Do you experience miracles in your life and run away excited to tell the world but forget to turn to Jesus to say "thank You"? Let's not take so much for granted that we forget to give our shouts of praise to Jesus for the things He gives us daily.

Father God, let me be the woman who always responds with praise and gratitude. I am so thankful for the daily wonders, moments of healing, and great love You show me. Amen.

Take Action

Be a woman who is known for her thank-yous. Read this prayer aloud and embrace the heart of gratitude it expresses.

Oh, Lord, I thank You for the privilege and gift of living in a world filled with beauty and excitement and variety...I thank You for the delights of music and children, of other people's thoughts and conversation and their books to read by the fireside or in bed with the rain falling on the roof or the snow blowing past outside the window. —Louis Bromfield

Your Reflections

_____

_____

_____

You Have a Firm Foundation

*Do not fear, for I am with you; do not anxiously
look about you, for I am your God. I will
strengthen you, surely I will help you, surely I will
uphold you with My righteous right hand
(Isaiah 41:10 NASB).*

As we live out life we must ask ourselves, what is our authority? A handshake is only as good as the person who shakes your hand. And that is the way it is in life. In today's verse we look at the content and say, "It's well and good, but who is this person who makes these promises?"

God's Word is a sufficient foundation for our faith. Here are a few selected promises from the Bible that will give you hope as you journey through life:

- Isaiah 41:10—Reread today's verse.

- Isaiah 43:2 (NASB)—When you pass through the waters, I will be with you; and through the rivers, they will not overflow you. When you walk through the fire, you will not be scorched, nor will the flame burn you.

- 2 Corinthians 12:9 (NASB)—My grace is sufficient for you, for power is perfected in weakness. Most gladly, therefore, I will rather boast about my weaknesses, that the power of Christ may dwell in me.

- Hebrews 13:5 (NASB)—I will never desert you, nor will I ever forsake you.

When God says it, you can take it to the bank. That's a handshake between you and Him.

> Father God, may my foundation be built on Your authority. If You say it, I believe. You are my salvation. Amen.

Take Action

If God says it, you can believe it. What is God saying to you through Scripture right now? Write that down and then spend time in prayer accepting the truth.

Your Reflections

_____

_____

_____

Who Is Your Potter?

Does not the potter have a right over the clay, to make
from the same lump one vessel for honorable use, and
another for common use? (Romans 9:21 NASB).

Recently we were visiting the lovely town of Carmel on the central coast of California. Since it's known to be a very artsy community we had plenty of opportunity to watch a variety of artists at work. We came upon this group of pottery makers demonstrating their craftsmanship. We soon observed that each of them started with a lump of clay to begin their project. Once it became more than a lump, the artist used different amounts of water and various hand pressures to form their work into an object.

Some creations were cups, some were bowls, and some were animals. Each artist had, in their mind, what their final display was going to be. For some the final project sold for $25 and some went as high as $200, but each object started out as a simple, formless lump of clay.

In pottery, the true beauty of the clay comes out after the firing in the kiln. The extreme heat produces a chemical reaction that causes the pottery to take on qualities it could never have without fire.

During your times of stress, challenge, or change, you can embrace what God is accomplishing in your life by allowing Him to take those rough spots in your experiences and your character and refine them into something of beauty. Think about a trial you have been through recently or even an ongoing struggle you face. Have you only considered it a burden? Try looking at it through the lens of a blessing. What about you is changing for the better? How is God using the current circumstances to lead you to His heart?

Do you see how you are being shaped into a prized woman of God because of a difficulty? Allow the Lord to continue molding and reshaping your beautiful vessel. Allow yourself to give the lump of an obstacle to God's capable, masterful hands.

Let Him make that into a piece of a priceless treasure. Let Him make you into fine porcelain.

Father God, take my lump of clay and mold me into who You want me to become. Add a little water here and a little finger pressure there to mold and shape me into a pleasing design. I thank You for letting me be the person that You can use in Your creation. Amen.

Take Action

Be willing to turn your life over to the Master Potter. Stop being rigid or you will easily break; stay pliable so you can be shaped in life.

Your Reflections

_____

_____

_____

God, I'm Calling You Today

*I will never desert you, nor will I ever
forsake you (Hebrews 13:5 NASB).*

We can read and hear about all the promises found in God's Word, but until we act on them they don't do us any good. I know that to be true in my everyday functions. The other day I was reading my car insurance benefits and I learned something new. They listed an 800 number that I could call if I needed tow service. Wow, that's a great benefit. I wrote that number down for future reference if I ever needed a towing. It's there, I believe, and I plan on acting upon that provision.

Every time I read God's Word, I learn something new. Even though I may have read it previously, I am able to grasp it as a promise that God has given me in a new way and for a new life situation. That is the power of the living Word. It is active and relevant *always*.

When I was diagnosed with cancer we were searching for a verse that could give us hope for this journey. A friend had written us a note expressing her prayers for us. At the end she had written down a verse of Scripture that became our theme song for our journey. It was, "This sickness is not unto death, but for the glory of God, that the Son of God may be glorified by it" (John 11:4 NASB).

There's something about pain that brings us down to the basics of who we are, what we can trust, and what is truly important. When your energy is limited, extraneous matters seem, well extraneous. There's nothing like suffering to make a person throw out what doesn't work and cling desperately to what proves real and true.

The one reality that stares me in the face whenever I'm hurting, is how much I need my heavenly Father to be near. First Peter 5:10 calls Him the God of all grace. In your own time of testing, if you keep yourself open to His working in your life, you will know that grace and that peace.

> Dear Lord, give me the faith to allow You to carry me through a difficult time in my life. I don't want to live life under my own strength. I want to trust You for my strength. I want You to be my first call in my moment of need. May I always see Your gentle touch on my life each day, dear Lord. You are the Master Gardener, tending to the garden of my soul. Amen.

Take Action

Claim a verse of Scripture that you can trust to give you strength for your time of testing. Tuck it into your purse or place it on the visor in your car.

Your Reflections

_____

_____

_____

Don't Let Robbers Steal Your Time

*The sluggard craves and gets nothing, but the desires
of the diligent are fully satisfied (Proverbs 13:4).*

When we are young, we aren't aware of the value of time. But as we get older we realize how valuable time is. We also realize that there doesn't seem to be enough of it—it is a limited resource and a precious one.

Each day I live, the less time I have. It is true for all of us. I don't mean that to be a depressing thought. If we embrace that knowledge as a powerful truth, we discover how valuable it is to be careful of the things we let into our lives that use up the commodity of time.

Failing to plan the day is one of the top time robbers. It goes right along with putting things off or trying to do everything yourself. It's time to get back to the basics: "If you fail to plan, you plan to fail." Start today to make it a priority to plan the day, before the day plans you. Promise less, deliver more. Remember, if you can't manage your time, you won't be able to manage any other part of your life.

Read and meditate on this wonderful paraphrase of Ephesians 5:16: "Time is a daily treasure that attracts many robbers!" There are many things that will steal your time and rob you of the focus you need to follow the Lord in the things He has called you to do. Be aware, you are protecting a valuable treasure.

Consider your life and your time are of great significance. God is working through both for His purposes. When you question the value of your days because they all seem the same, remember that each morning is providing for you a clean slate of opportunity to do what counts.

Set aside at least an hour of personal time to replenish your body, your mind, and your soul. Let the Lord give you discipline to break bad habits of neglect and develop new ones of healthy concern and responsibility.

Father God, let me be able to discern the robber barons in my life. I want to protect my valuable time so I have time to be able to do for You what I need to. Help me to feel generous of spirit and heart when I give to others and give to You. I don't want to be selfish or reluctant to follow Your leading. Amen.

Take Action

Make a to-do list each evening for your activities the next day. Rank them by priority. Do the first things first. Give yourself grace when you have to let go of the other things.

Your Reflections

_____

_____

_____

You Are a Star!

"For I know the plans I have for you," declares the
LORD, "plans to prosper you and not to harm you, plans
to give you hope and a future" (Jeremiah 29:11).

Have you ever wanted to be a star? I think the glamour and adventure could be fun, but when I look at the magazines on the grocery store racks and see their lives picked apart or magnified, I realize that I am very glad to be me. And you can be very glad that you are you.

Have you ever thought that you're a star people can touch? Does your life light up the room when you enter? Do your children or grandchildren reflect back the love you give them? Do you brighten the office and the lives of your coworkers as you start the day?

Each one of us has to start with a new twenty-four hours every day. Each one of us has seven days in every week. What are you doing with your days and hours? What are your deepest dreams? Writing a novel, singing a song in front of others, pursuing a new job? Starting a new company? Your life is a star. Don't let that star fall to the ground and don't underestimate the power of its light. As you begin each day, plan to nurture and water your dreams until the "Sonlight" makes them grow.

It is no small thing to be a light and to reflect God's love. Consider how you can best illuminate your life and your family's life by directing everyone to the one source of goodness, salvation, and purpose.

Someone once said, "Make big plans; aim high in hope and work." The Bible says in Philippians 3:14 (NASB): "Press on toward the goal for the prize of the upward call of God in Christ Jesus." Then remember to be on the lookout for those other stars around you. Your encouragement and affirmation can make a big difference for their dreams too.

Lord, thanks for making me the right kind of star. I'm so happy to be me. Your Son makes me light up every time I'm around His people. Help me to shine. Help me to use my days for Your glory. Amen.

Take Action

This little light of mine, I'm going to let it shine; hide it under a bushel, no. I'm going to let it shine.

Your Reflections

_____

_____

_____

Growing in God Through Our Problems

We can rejoice, too, when we run into problems and trials, for we know that they are good for us—they help us learn to be patient. And patience develops strength of character in us and helps us trust God more each time we use it until finally our hope and faith are strong and steady (Romans 5:3-4 TLB).

There are significant benefits that arise out of our struggles. Our verse today creates a list of ways that our trials become blessings and benefits as they:

1. help us learn patience
2. develop our patience into strength of character
3. help us trust God more each time we are patient
4. build up our hope and faith

The problems we face will either defeat us or they will develop us to become what God wants us to be. We often cry out, "I don't need this problem!" when, in reality, it's just what we need. Over the years, I've learned basic principles to help me understand why problems exist:

To give us guidance. Problems often point us in a different and new direction and motivate us to change. Sometimes it takes a painful situation to redirect our steps.

To inspect us. As an impatient person, I had to be inspected. I had to make adjustments when my faults were exposed. Problems cause you to inspect who you really are.

To correct us. Sometimes we only learn the value of something—health, money, a career, a relationship—by losing it. Change or be changed.

To protect us. Often one problem protects us from experiencing a larger problem later. Trust that God has a plan and purpose for every experience given to us. (See Jeremiah 29:11.)

To perfect us. God is more interested in our character than our comfort. When we measure our success, we not only measure our achievements but we measure lessons learned, lives touched, and moments shared along the way. God perfects us and shapes us through difficult times.

Lord, let me have a fuller appreciation of how to handle my problems. Or better yet, how to give my problems to You and then learn the lessons You offer me in my trials. Give me the faith, courage, and energy to see the long-term value of my problems. Thanks for caring for me. Amen.

Take Action

Turn your problems into real learning experiences. Don't look down—look up. Take time today to consider which struggles or problems in your past have been your greatest teachers.

Your Reflections

_____

_____

_____

Making Your Empty Tank Full

Elijah was a man with a nature like
ours (James 5:17 NASB).

The feeling of running on empty is very common for women today. We put a lot of pressure on ourselves. And the journey, although filled with great moments, can also be filled with so many demands, detours, and very little rest. And sometimes we feel like we keep going along, trying our best, and it just isn't enough to ever feel replenished, let alone caught up.

When you get depleted, it is easy to question if you are walking in God's purpose for you and whether you will ever feel energized in the way you are going. Elijah of the Bible felt just like that. He was running on empty.

- verse 2—He was being threatened to have life taken.
- verse 3—He was afraid.
- verse 4—He prayed that he might die.
- verse 5—He was touched by an angel, who said, "Arise, eat."
- verse 9—He was asked by the Lord, "What are you doing here?"
- verses 11-12—He was confronted by strong winds, an earthquake, a fire, and a sound of gentle blowing (a gentle whisper).
- verse 14—He told the Lord he had done all the Lord had asked and that he alone was left.

Yes, Elijah was human, just like we are. He was threatened, he was alone, he wanted to die, he was confused, he wanted to give in and call it quits. But he didn't. He went on top of the mountain. In verses 11-12 he heard the sound of a gentle whisper. He could have ignored the message, but he didn't. By wise counsel from the Lord, Elijah was assured that he wasn't done (verses 15-16), he wasn't alone (verse 16), he wasn't a failure (verse 18).

If you find yourself in that empty state like Elijah, you can be assured that you're not done, not alone, and not a failure. Listen to the gentle whisper and get back on track.

Father God, lift me out of a life of emptiness. I know this is not where I will remain. With Your Spirit and power I will rise above this phase of emptiness and live an abundant life. Thank You for gently whispering into my heart. Amen.

Take Action

If you find yourself running on empty, stop and rest. Find ways to restore your energy. Seek out a friend or group of friends that will help you during this dry season of life.

Your Reflections

_____

_____

_____

Hearing the "Whisper of God"

What are you doing here, Elijah? (1 Kings 19:13).

Have you ever been in a situation and a still small voice whispers, "What are you doing here"? Over a lifetime we can hear this voice and this question numerous times. You can ignore it or you can stop in your tracks and listen to God as He challenges you in your present situation.

We grow spiritually when we take the time to pause and listen to what God is asking of us. If we miss these moments because we are too busy or we avoid them because we are reluctant to find out what God is teaching us, we become stuck in life and in faith.

Scripture gives us four ways to get away so we can hear the whisper of God's voice:

1. *Go to a quiet spot.* "Very early in the morning, while it was still dark, Jesus got up, left the house and went off to a solitary place, where he prayed" (Mark 1:35).

2. *Have an open heart and God will listen.* "Call upon me and come and pray to me, and I will listen to you" (Jeremiah 29:12).

3. *Open your Bible.* "The word of God is living and active. Sharper than any double-edged sword, it penetrates even to dividing soul and spirit, joints and marrow; it judges the thoughts and attitudes of the heart" (Hebrews 4:12).

4. *Have a genuine friend.* "Let us consider how we may spur one another on toward love and good deeds. Let us not give up meeting together, as some are in the habit of doing, but let us

encourage one another—and all the more as you see the Day approaching" (Hebrews 10:24-25).

God has not meant our lives to be empty or directionless. He leads us, encourages us, and offers us a way through life that is rewarding and fruitful. His plan is for us to live full and abundant lives. Walk with and in the purpose God has for you. You and those in your life will be richly blessed.

God, give me the desire to live a life with purpose. I don't want to just keep digging a deeper hole. Let my ears hear Your whisper as You guide me, nudge me, and show me the way to walk in Your purpose and plan for my life. Amen.

Take Action

When God speaks, stop what you are doing and listen to His voice, even when it is a gentle whisper. I encourage you to journal during these times to note what insights arise during your quiet time with God.

Your Reflections

_____

_____

_____

Two Are Better than One

A cord of three strands is not quickly torn
apart (Ecclesiastes 4:12 NASB).

Help is on the way. We live in a world where I think a lot of us feel pressure to say, "I can do it myself." However, that's one of the lies of our day. God placed Adam and Eve together. He knew they would need each other. It was true then and it is true today. A load is always lighter when you have someone to help you.

Because we believe this lie that we are to do things only in our power, we forget to ask others to help us out. And then how often do we secretly complain when we don't receive the help we think we deserve? Do you see how that is a no-win situation? God doesn't want us to go through that cycle of hoping for help, withholding our request for help, and then being disappointed when we struggle alone in our circumstances.

Our truest help starts from within ourselves. When we have a heart that relies on God and trusts His provision, we learn the value of co-laboring through life with Him and, in turn, with others. Although we need to dig in and do our own work, sometimes we do need the help of others. King Solomon in all his wisdom tells us that friends are great blessings to us:

- Woe to the one who falls when there is not another to lift him up (Ecclesiastes 4:10 NASB).

- If two lie down together they keep warm (Ecclesiastes 4:11 NASB).

- If one can overpower him who is alone, two can resist him (Ecclesiastes 4:12 NASB).

- A cord of three strands is not quickly torn apart (Ecclesiastes 4:12 NASB).

Are you working on relationships that build these blessings? Begin at home with your family members. Throughout Scripture we are reminded to be united, to be of the same spirit, to be of one accord. Unity should be our goal. Don't be afraid to ask for help and certainly be available to help others. We learn so much about God when we team up.

Father God, let me see the need to not only ask for help, but be willing to offer help. I want to experience the importance of togetherness. I want to share in this life and faith journey with Your other children. Amen.

Take Action

Start seeking the gift of help by tending to your own heart. In your quiet time, take your needs to the Lord. Ask for His help and answers. Now take that willingness to ask for help and to share in life to your spouse, your family, and to your neighbors.

Your Reflections

Why Do You Do What You Do?

Do not be overrighteous, neither be overwise—
why destroy yourself? (Ecclesiastes 7:16).

You've heard the old saying "Don't be so heavenly minded that you are no earthly good." A helpful key word to live by is "moderation." Once you reach a certain level in a material way, what more can you do? You don't need more than three meals a day. You can't wear two outfits at the same time or more than one pair of shoes. You only need one car to get around, if even that. We do have a neighbor with nine cars spread out over three residences. So people have their areas of indulgence most definitely! But if, for your life, you look at what you really need, you understand that there is very little you must have to be healthy, happy, and able to fulfill life as God's stewards.

One way to make sure that fame and fortune don't change you is to keep in mind that you're allotted only so much time on this earth—neither money nor celebrity will buy you a couple of extra years. If you've ever been through a tough medical journey or accompanied someone through that, you are reminded again and again how fragile and precious life is. Those extras that the world applauds mean so little when you are embracing the gift of another day and the joy of relationship with the Lord.

Life is so complicated that it's hard for anyone to figure out what their purpose in life is and to whom they are accountable. If we understand that our main priority is to love God, know God, and walk with Him, we will always be certain to stay accountable to the One we are born to be accountable to!

When we're young, we often think we know all the answers in life. But as we get older we begin to realize that we fit into a master plan that can't always be explained. If we stay true to a vow of moderation as we stay close to God's heart, there is great joy and purpose ahead. You won't have to look back on life with regrets of excess or destructive tangents.

King Solomon realized that God has a sovereign purpose, and that He doesn't always reveal to us the key to His plan. By what authority do you do what you do? There lies the answer to life. What are you living for?

Father God, humble my spirit so that I might be open to new truths today that I might better understand the whys of life. You know that I want to expand my mind to be more like You! Amen.

Take Action

Under the heading "Your Reflections" list several of your "why" questions. Realize that you will not always know the answer to these whys. Turn these questions over to God in prayer and give them up to Him.

Your Reflections

_____

_____

_____

Commandments of Marriage

*You will seek me and find me when you seek
me with all your heart (Jeremiah 29:13).*

Bob and I have been together many wonderful years. Were they all easy? Absolutely not. Were they all filled with lessons on love and commitment? Yes! If you're married, you know just what I mean. And even when we are single, we learn so much about ourselves and the way of commitment and faithfulness by the way we interact with others.

Throughout our years of marriage, we have made several observations about what it takes to have a successful marriage. We call them our "Ten Commandments of Marriage." In this devotion and the next, I will summarize those commandments. I pray they will be of help and encouragement to you.

1. *Be affectionate.* Every day your spouse needs many hugs to reaffirm your love for each other. Not only must you be a hugger, you must be a teller. You must tell each other that you love them and give each other a compliment each day.

2. *Engage in conversation.* Women seem to need this more than men do. But our husbands also need a chance to share their hopes and wants. It's important that both parties learn how to listen and to be present for one another with compassion.

3. *Be transparent.* Open up and be honest with each other. Be an encourager so your husband feels safe when opening up. And share what is on your heart rather than holding it back and hoping that your husband can read your mind.

4. *Prioritize your finances.* Proper money management is an ingredient for a healthy marriage. Create a plan for spending and saving and approach money as a team.

5. *Shine in your role.* God designed each marriage partner to play a particular role in having a healthy family. Each family has to decide how those roles are played out to best benefit and unite the family. There are sacrifices that must be made in a family.

Take Action

This week, do something proactive in each of these five commandment categories! Watch how that one action leads to positive results. Remember that God gave us two ears and only one mouth...so we are to listen twice as much as we speak.

Your Reflections

_____

_____

_____

More Marriage Commandments

*Two are better than one, because they have a
good return for their work (Ecclesiastes 4:9).*

Today, let's keep exploring the "commandments" Bob and I have
found to be helpful guidelines and encouragements toward commitment in our marriage. We just looked at 1-5, so let's move on to 6-10.
As you go through these, think about which ones are easy for you and
which are difficult. Ask God for His help.

6. *Pursue a healthy sex life.* Devote time to romance and sexual
   activity. Express affection and tenderness throughout the
   day. Create a "date night" to allow you and your husband
   to connect in conversation and laughter. Hold hands and
   snuggle on the couch. Intimacy strengthens a couple.

7. *Invest in companionship.* When your spouse becomes your
   best friend it pays rich dividends. Support each other's
   interests. Whenever possible seek out common interests
   to enjoy together. There are many healthy ways that we
   can fulfill this commandment: go out to dinner regularly,
   vacation together, go to the theater, take walks together,
   attend church functions, and so on.

8. *Remain attractive to one another.* I'm not suggesting we
   add pressure to be perfect. However, remaining attractive
   to our spouse is a way to show we care. Isn't it nice when
   your husband is willing to try a new shirt you got him or
   when you wear a dress that you know is your husband's
   favorite color? When one of you isn't feeling good about

your appearance, let the other be a mirror which reflects unconditional love. Build up the confidence of one another.

9. *Be a team on the home front.* Most women adore a husband who helps with the household chores! Make a plan to assign certain chores to family members. Domestic support needs to be shared by everyone. And approaching home management as a team leads to unity and fun.

10. *Admire and appreciate each other.* We all want to feel worthy of what we do. Take time to express thankfulness for your husband. Train your children how to express their thanks to you both as parents by developing in them a heart of gratitude. A hug and a thank-you go a long way.

Lord, thank You for helping to make our home such a "welcome center." May these "Ten Commandments" be a starting place to help make our marriage a strong model for others to see. Help us to invest time in our relationship so that we never take each other for granted and we become a source of inspiration and encouragement to one another. Amen.

Take Action

Take one commandment a week for the next ten weeks and try to strengthen these areas of your marriage. Share about your experience with your spouse or work through them at the same time!

Your Reflections

_____

_____

_____

There Is Strength in Togetherness

*For I am confident of this very thing, that He who
began a good work in you will perfect it until the
day of Christ Jesus (Philippians 1:6 NASB).*

When we truly long to grow as Christians, we need to devote time
and attention to how we nurture our minds, hearts, and our actions.
As we seek God's leading and guidance to shape our minds and hearts,
the fruit of our actions becomes more righteous and good. When we
go to God's Word, He has many directives to help us with these areas.

Mind

While the world offers us many things we shouldn't give our mental energy to, God directs us to what will fill us with His best and will
help us mature as Christian women. "Whatever is true, whatever
is honorable, whatever is right, whatever is pure, whatever is lovely,
whatever is of good repute, if there is any excellence and if anything
worthy of praise, dwell on these things" (Philippians 4:8 NASB).

Heart

Psalm 26:2 reads, "Test me, O LORD, and try me, examine my
heart and my mind." Each of us needs this verse as our battle cry. We
will never know who we are or who we can become unless we are willing to be tested. If you bring your heart before the Lord and ask for
Him to examine it, you can then redirect your heart to be in line with
God. Head knowledge will not save us. We have to go from the head
to the heart—which is approximately sixteen inches—to make the
change in our mind-set.

Actions

God empowers us to walk in His ways. And when we are unsure what to do or how to respond to a situation, He reminds us to go back to the basics of godly living: "What does the LORD require of you? To act justly and to love mercy and to walk humbly with your God" (Micah 6:8).

Father God, I want You to work in my life. I want to become the woman You long for me to be. Examine my mind and heart. Show me where I need to seek You more fully so that I can live out my faith with daily choices and actions that bring glory to You. Amen.

Take Action

Examine your own heart to see what work is needed for your Christian growth. If you have a friend of faith, consider asking her to help you stay accountable to godly thoughts, beliefs, and actions. Seek to fill any sense of void or lack with God's truth and promises.

Your Reflections

_____

_____

_____

Why Me, Lord?

We know that in all things God works for the
good of those who love him, who have been called
according to his purpose (Romans 8:28).

Have you ever asked the question, "Why me, Lord?" When I was first diagnosed with cancer, I had all kinds of questions cross my mind. However, from past experiences in difficult situations I knew that nothing comes to us before it first comes through God's screening process. The secular world doesn't know this principle. As believers, though, we can be at peace when trials come our way.

Sometimes we wonder why God lets us go through such bad and difficult times, but we know that when He puts things in His order, they always work for good. We just have to trust Him—and eventually they will all make something wonderful! Of course, it isn't always easy to trust, but I can tell you from experience that your faith will deepen like never before when God accompanies you through a trial of significance. I can honestly say that God shaped me into an even more faithful, grateful person during my struggles because He was with me every day.

When I look back on the life I have lived so far and some of the stresses God has brought me through, I want to praise Him. I want to give Him glory. And I want each day from here on out to be devoted to serving my faithful Lord.

A stone has to come under a lot of pressure before it can become a precious diamond. When I cry out to God to have Him get rid of the pain in my life He responds, "Not yet."

What trial have you faced? What pressure are you under that you have wished away? Try bringing it to God with full faith that He will help you through the circumstances and that He will shape you into a precious treasure even through what the world might view as an unredeemable loss or pain. You are not alone, my friend. Our God is with you and He sees the gem you are becoming.

> Father God, life isn't easy. Help me to trust You in everything. Give me a trusting spirit that leans into Your Word and Your guidance with faithfulness. I might not understand all that I am facing, but I know that each trial is another opportunity to witness Your compassion, care, and redemption. Amen.

Take Action

Don't say "Why me, Lord?" Instead, say "Why not me?" God is in this situation with you and He is for you. You are not left to go this road alone.

Your Reflections

_____

_____

_____

Who Are You?

God said to Moses, "I AM WHO I AM" (Exodus 3:14).

We live in a world where people are continually looking to find out who they are. Many divorced couples say they are leaving the marriage to find out who they are, and adopted children search earnestly to find their biological parents so they can better know who they are. Right in front of each of us is Scripture that tells us who we are. We don't have to search the world to find out who we are when the Bible assures us of our heritage and our eternity.

Take time to read the following to find out who you are to our Lord. If God said it, you can believe it:

> I am God's child. (John 1:12)
>
> I am confident that God will perfect the work He has begun in me. (Philippians 1:6)
>
> I am a citizen of heaven. (Philippians 3:20)
>
> I am a light to others. (Ephesians 5:8-9)
>
> I have not been given a spirit of fear, but of power, love, and self-discipline. (2 Timothy 1:7)
>
> I am given God's glorious grace. (Ephesians 1:5,7)
>
> I am forgiven. (Colossians 1:14)
>
> I am a new creation. (2 Corinthians 5:17)

Until we really get to know how to worship God we aren't able to know who He is. We can look around at all of His creation and enjoy the beauty, but that's not the same as knowing Him. The more that we know God, the more we appreciate who He really is and the gift of being His. And the more we appreciate who He really is, the more motivated we will be to bring Him glory.

One of the most amazing things about knowing God is that He shares with us who He is. Scripture tells us that He even shares His power with us, knowing His will gives us purpose for living. He does all of this because He loves us—enough to forgive us of all our sins. The cross made it possible.

God, thank You for letting me know You better. Through this I am able to accept who I am. I appreciate Your revelation throughout Scripture. When life becomes busy, I do feel that I can lose myself and my connection to You. Help me to seek You out and to tend to my heart and spirit in times of quiet and stillness so that I may know You better and more fully. Amen.

Take Action

Take time to study these Scripture verses so you can know who God is and who you are as His daughter. Consider writing a letter to God as you would write a letter from a daughter to her father. Tell Him what is going on in your life.

Your Reflections

_____

_____

_____

You Are Known by Your Choices

*If any of you lacks wisdom, let him ask of God, who
gives to all generously and without reproach, and
it will be given to him (James 1:5 NASB).*

The Bible is full of wonderful assurances and promises for all who
believe in Jesus Christ, the Son of God. Reflect on how these promises can be yours. The Bible says:

- *Recognize* you cannot be saved by trying to be good or
  by doing good. "By grace you have been saved through
  faith; and that not of yourselves, it is the gift of God; not
  as a result of works, so that no one may boast" (Ephesians
  2:8-9 NASB).

- *Confess* that you are a sinner worthy of God's righteous
  judgment, and that you are hopelessly lost without the
  Lord Jesus Christ as your personal Savior. "If you confess
  with your mouth Jesus as Lord, and believe in your heart
  that God raised Him from the dead, you shall be saved;
  for with the heart a person believes, resulting in righteousness, and with the mouth he confesses, resulting in
  salvation" (Romans 10:9-10 NASB).

- *Believe* the good news that Jesus died for you and set-
  tled your sin debt by His death on the cross. Believe that
  Christ was raised from the dead and now lives to save all
  who will come to Him in faith. "[Jesus] is able also to save
  forever those who draw near to God through Him, since

He always lives to make intercession for them" (Hebrews 7:25 NASB).

- *Call* on the name of the Lord Jesus Christ with a sincere desire to be saved from your sins. God has promised that "everyone who calls on the name of the Lord will be saved" (Romans 10:13).

- *Rely* upon God's sure promises, not upon your feelings. Openly confess Him as your Lord and Savior. "God so loved the world, that He gave His only begotten Son, that whoever believes in Him should not perish, but have eternal life" (John 3:16 NASB).

If you have never put your faith in Jesus as your personal Savior, I encourage you to do it right now in the quietness of your own heart.

Father God, I realize I'm a sinner and separated from You. I open my heart to receive You as my personal Savior and Lord of my life. I know You will forgive me of my sins. I want You to be my mentor and to give me guidance and purpose for life. I want You to be the Potter, and I will be the clay. Mold me and make me in Your own way. Amen.

Take Action

I encourage you to think through these actions several times this week as you pray to God with gratitude.

Your Reflections

_____

_____

_____

Let Go of Your Fears

We do not have a high priest who cannot sympathize
with our weaknesses, but One who has been tempted in
all things as we are, yet without sin (Hebrews 4:15 NASB).

We are so blessed. Our Savior is sympathetic to our human experience and does not abandon us in our trials. We can look back at our struggles and examine current ones and know that God does understand. This assurance and peace can encourage us to live our days with faith rather than fear.

Jesus endured pain and suffering, and He can now offer us mercy and grace to help in our time of need. Our verse today helps me trust and love Him all the more. He cares because He understands our temptations.

The passage in Hebrews 4:14-16 tells us to hold on to our faith (what we believe). This High Priest of ours understands our weaknesses, because He faced all of the same testings we do, yet He did not sin. So let us come boldly to the throne of our gracious God. There we will receive His mercy, and we will find grace to help us when we need it most.

- *Mercy* is the undeserved favor that forgives us.
- *Grace* is the unearned favor that saves us.

In the book of Exodus we are able to read and witness the struggle that Moses had with God. Early on, he told God he wasn't good enough (he was fearful). In Exodus 4:13 we read that Moses told God to please send someone else. In the end we read that Moses said "yes" to God and started trusting Him with faith. If Moses had not said "Yes," he would have missed all that God had for him.

We too have to trust God if we are going to be what God wants us to become. Maybe you are in a situation right now that causes you to doubt or be afraid rather than trust. Listen closely to God as He says, "You can trust Me." Believe it and move forward with faith.

Jesus, guide my steps through my troubles and my temptations. Help me to hold tightly to my faith and beliefs so that I do not turn from Your best for me. I trust You with my situation, my day, and my future. I am so grateful. Amen.

Take Action

Write down a prayer in which you give all of your current temptations and trials to God. As you do this, think of Him holding you and guiding you through these circumstances.

Your Reflections

_____

_____

_____

Be at Peace in Sleep

Cast your cares upon the Lord *and he
will sustain you (Psalm 55:22).*

Have you ever tossed and turned because you are worrying about some issue in life? Perhaps you worry about a child, work pressures, or financial burdens? Whatever it is, it keeps replaying itself in your head. You fret and stare at the ceiling at night. And during the day, you lose your train of thought and your breathing becomes shallow as anxiety lingers.

When those stressful thoughts creep into your mind, think on today's psalm so you can have peace. When God says to cast your burden upon Him and He will sustain you, He means every word of that promise. Remember, God is not capable of breaking His promises.

A valley will get you very close to God. I'm not sure why we wait until a problem arrives, but think about how quickly we seek God when problems arise. That is when we are really needy for God's comfort. As a parent, we anxiously await the time our children come and talk to us. We do best when we stay connected. Think about how much God wants us to come and talk to Him.

I've meekly prayed; I've prayed with anger, with tears, with petitions, with despair, with praise, and of course with thanksgiving. God has heard me each time and He has sustained me. He has been good in the past and now in the present and I know He will be there for my future.

He will sustain you too. Not only that, He will work out the problem that's plaguing you, no matter what it is. God delights in being our God. Don't rob Him of the joy He gets from shouldering your burden for you.

He truly wants to help. Prepare the way for your communication with Him by praying during all circumstances. Nothing is too big or too small to bring before the Lord. Don't wait for an emergency to call.

Father God, help me to break my cycle of worry. When I am restless in mind and spirit, may I turn to Your Word and to Your presence for my peace. Guide my thoughts so that they come from You and are not reflections of fear. I want faith, not fear, to rule my life, Lord. Amen.

Take Action

Writing down our worries and giving them to God in some form of ceremony can be very freeing. Jot down worries and then place them in an envelope marked "In God's care." Consider how good it feels to know that your concerns are in God's hands now.

Your Reflections

_____

_____

_____

No Busy Signals in Heaven

Give ear to my prayer, O God, and do not hide
Yourself from my supplication (Psalm 55:21 NKJV).

God always hears us. When we lift up our voice, our thoughts, our spirit's cries, He listens. There are never any busy signals and there are no numbers to punch. That's a lifetime guarantee. It's free—no service charges or federal or state taxes.

As I approach God in either public or private prayer, I must remember that this is an appointed time between me and my Lord. I must not use flowery speech or feel the need to be elaborate and perfect in front of those who hear me talk with God. Jesus shared His approach to prayer to the disciples through the Lord's Prayer (Matthew 6:9-13), and that is a perfect example of how we are to pray and how we are to pray when with others. We need to be humble as we approach and worship the Lord.

Over the years Bob and I have had the opportunity and privilege of having many, many people praying for us. We have always been so blessed when those who came to visit asked, "Would you mind if I prayed for you?" "Of course not," came our immediate reply.

Often the most powerful prayers were those uttered by God-fearing, humble warriors of the faith. Many of these were people who had traveled down the same road we have traveled. They understood the suffering we were experiencing. They knew that words spoken before the Lord on our behalf can soothe the hurts of any illness or struggle. From years of their own valleys they were quick to go directly to God and place their burdens at the foot of the cross. He hears and responds with a blessing. Each petition has an impact upon our heavenly Father. He listens with an open ear to those who are lowly in spirit.

Commit to being a prayer warrior for a friend in need. If you are concerned about praying aloud for the person, use a verse of the Lord's Prayer to become more comfortable with this act of faith. The petitions and praises of your heart will soon rise up in your prayers and the words will flow with greater ease. God never asks for a perfect prayer. Your open line to Him is your open and willing heart.

Father God, I come before You with a humble heart. I ask for the words to speak on behalf of my friend in need. You know what she needs long before she does or I do…direct my heart and spirit so that I can lift her up in prayer and be a spiritual companion for her now and in the days ahead. Amen.

Take Action

Memorize the Lord's Prayer and say it out loud each day in your quiet time. It will become a great source of comfort to you and to those you share it with.

Your Reflections

_____

_____

_____

Abide and Remain

*Just as the Father has loved Me, I have also loved
you; abide in My love (John 15:9 NASB).*

Christianity is not a religion; Christianity is a relationship. When I
first heard that many years ago, I was somewhat concerned, because
I always considered that Christianity was one of the great religions of
the world. That was until I realized that my walk was with Jesus and
that I was no longer under the law of the Old Testament, but under
the grace of the New Testament.

Religion has a set of rules that one must obey. Religion says, "You
ought to do this and you should not do that. If you do, you will be
punished." Have you come to the same realization I have, that you
just can't live up to this long list of rules? The moment we figure this
out can be our moment of great freedom and faith. We realize that we
are called to a relationship with our Savior. And what we can do is all
in His strength. Our default might be to turn from relationship and
back toward rules. Structure can feel safe sometimes...safer than faith
and trust. But in and through relationship with Christ, we have much
more freedom. The apostle Paul wrote in Romans 6:14, "For sin shall
not be your master, because you are not under law, but under grace."
What a powerful truth for us today. So how do we rest in this when
we try but fail to follow the old law? Two thoughts can become our
foundation for action: abide in His love, remain in His love.

Paul tells us in Galatians 5:16-19 that if we walk by the Spirit, we
will not carry out the desires of the flesh. The Spirit and the flesh are in
conflict. If you are led by the Spirit, you are not under the law. Since
we live by the Spirit, let us keep in step with the Spirit. If the Spirit

is our focus in life, we won't be concerned by what we shouldn't be doing, but under grace and what flows out of us (verses 22-23): love, joy, peace, patience, kindness, goodness, faithfulness, gentleness, and self-control.

Lord of grace, You have given to me a path of mercy to follow. In Your strength, I can live a righteous life that is not about rules but is about relationship. My faith deepens each time I fall into Your arms and trust that You are there. My hope brightens each time I step forward and acknowledge that You are leading the way. Amen.

Take Action

As you go about your day and week, pay attention to which fruits of the Spirit are evident in your life. Consider which are less evident and give those areas to God in full trust and faith. See what unfolds!

Your Reflections

_____

_____

_____

Knowing God in Stillness

Be still, and know that I am God (Psalm 46:10).

Our culture is severely overstimulated. Loud music at home, at the mall, and even at most restaurants. Advertisements fill everything we read, hear, and see. Even activities that are our pleasures can be packed with noise, images, or distractions. If you enjoy surfing the Internet, watching movies, or posting or following posts via social media, you might suddenly realize that the afternoon has slipped away and you feel a bit more scattered than you did before.

No wonder so many people these days are nervous, have short attention spans, have hearing problems, and have a difficult time being still. Do we even bother to make room for stillness, quietness, and silence anymore? Do we take moments for reflection and rest so that we can clear our heads and talk to God?

I believe that even for those of us who do like quiet time with the Lord, the initial absence of sound or distraction can feel uncomfortable. We can be uneasy because it isn't natural. When I've attended a church service where there is a devoted time of silence, I have sensed the unease and the awkwardness in people around me. All of a sudden the adults become like children, squirming and fidgeting. We are that removed from the act of stillness!

Our culture is missing out on something great and important. Quiet times are refreshing to the soul, offering us reflection, perhaps a chance to mourn or to be happy or maybe even to hear God speak to us in a still, small voice.

Do such times exist in your home? Or is your house filled with the discordant sounds of television and pop music? Is it any wonder that many of us and our children do not know how to cultivate silence?

Our hearts and souls are longing for such peace, but we cover up that longing with more noise, more activity, and more distractions. Allow yourself the joy of pure silence and the treasure of prayer. Teach these gifts to your children. The psalmist knew that in order to know God, we have to stop striving and become still. The business of life must come to a halt in order to know God.

Father God, I find myself anxious; help me establish a quiet time each day so I can be still. In this stillness let me ponder who You are and may I know You in a greater way. Help me to establish my home as a place of peace, not electronic discord. Amen.

Take Action

Come to an agreement as a family that you will choose twenty-four hours once a week when all electronic equipment will be turned off. If that feels overwhelming, start with a four-hour window and add an hour every week. Turn it into time to talk, play games, get outside, and be together as a family.

Your Reflections

_____

_____

_____

Believing in God for the Future

O my soul, why be so gloomy and discouraged?
Trust in God! (Psalm 43:5 TLB).

I love the older, more mature believers because they have endless stories to tell how God has been faithful in the past, in the present, and they know He will take care of them in the future. You can gather so much hope and wisdom when you hear of another's journey with God over the years or through a particularly difficult season.

I become upset when I try to do things in my own power and strength. I might be going along well in faith and then something gets in the way. *I* get in the way. And I become discouraged. Can you relate to that?

In today's Scripture, the psalmist is expressing the same idea. Oh, soul, why be discouraged? Why be upset when you have God to trust? Then the psalmist continues: "I shall again praise him for his wondrous help; he will make me smile again, for he is my God!" When your spirit becomes gloomy, you must trust God continually.

Despite what's happening in our lives, we can say loud and clear, "We will not fear!" I encourage you to use some quiet time today or within the next week to go to God's Word and seek His assurance and comfort. Find a passage to memorize that gives you strength and is a reminder to trust Him more. The next time you are afraid or are just frustrated with your human failings, you will hear God's words in your heart and mind. These memorized verses will come to you just as you need them and they will remind you who is in charge.

I can believe that God will take care of me for the future because He has taken such good care of me in the past. If you struggle to see how God has held you up and guided you in the past, take time to listen to the faith stories of others. Take time to immerse yourself in the faith stories of Scripture. These shared journeys of God's faithfulness will not only inspire you but will illuminate ways in which God has been a part of your healing and your story all along.

> Father God, You are my source of strength. Lately, I am so discouraged by my own behavior and failings. I give them over to You. Make them into things of beauty. Things that serve You. Remind me that each time I fail or struggle is also a time I can lean on You with full assurance that You are there. Amen.

Take Action

Put your faith in action for today in a specific way. Pay attention to how God moves in the circumstance and through your time of trusting Him.

Your Reflections

_____

_____

_____

Accentuate the Positive

*When a man is gloomy, everything seems to
go wrong; when he is cheerful, everything
seems right! (Proverbs 15:15 TLB).*

Proverbs is such a great book to learn the facts of life. When I read through the thirty-one chapters I'm overwhelmed with what I learn. In fact every verse is full of wisdom. Have you ever thought about how wisdom in God counters negativity? When we are continually being told what we can't do or are even telling ourselves what we can't do, we are denying God's wisdom and perspective! We miss out on what is possible with God because we are stuck examining our circumstance through the lens of "If only."

- If only I didn't have this illness.
- If only I had a better job.
- If only my parents were still alive.
- If only I hadn't married my spouse.
- If only I had more education.
- If only I could win the lottery.

If only, if only, if only. The list could go on and on. This kind of thinking will keep us from being the person God wants us to be. We will either always be waiting for everything to line up perfectly before we act with faith or we will use our list as a list of excuses why we didn't act in faith. Faith isn't about waiting for all things to line up...faith is about lining up with God's will. Don't let your negative conversation drain the life from those around you or pull the plug on your dreams and purpose. Turn your "if only" into an "I can!" You can with God's strength. You can with God's leading. You can with God's blessing.

> Lord, infuse me with Your strength and guide me in positive, good works and thoughts. When I am tempted to turn to my list of "If onlys" direct my mind to Your Word and promises. There I will rediscover the perspective of hope and possibility. You are the God of possibilities. I want to live with Your perspective all the days of my life. Amen.

Take Action

Draw a line down the middle of a piece of paper. Now list your "If onlys" on one side and then turn them into "I cans" on the other side. Notice how encouraged and uplifted you feel as you shift your thinking to an "I can" mode.

Your Reflections

_____

_____

_____

How Does Your Garden Grow?

Yes, I am the Vine; you are the branches. Whoever lives
in me and I in him shall produce a large crop of fruit.
For apart from me you can't do a thing (John 15:5 TLB).

It is a well-known biblical principle: Whatever we sow, we reap. The harvest always comes after the planting. All other things being equal, we can anticipate that with good weather and adequate rain, we will produce a good crop if we have made the effort to prepare the soil and sow healthy seeds in the first place. This is true in our life. We will produce a good life and we will serve a good purpose when we have made the effort to tend to our spiritual soil and sowing.

One place where we can clearly see the result of our efforts is in the health and strength of our friendships. To this day, I am reaping the results of friendship seeds sown in previous seasons. I remember busy times when I didn't have time for friends—when a phone call, an email, a note, a lunch date, or even a word of prayer was truly a sacrifice of my time, when making time for others was truly a struggle. I thought I was too busy to plant those seeds of friendship.

I'm so thankful that I woke up to what was important in life. My selfishness almost prevented me from reaping the fruit of the future harvest. As I get older I'm so glad that I turned around my priorities and made an effort to sow seeds of friendship. Now I have the privilege of reaping an abundant harvest. I am so blessed to have all my family, friends, and loved ones around me during this time of my life. Through their expressions of love and kindness, they have shared Christ with me.

Today, be encouraged to plant your own seeds of friendship.

Express your love and kindness to someone today—with a phone call, a note, an email, or in person.

God, You have shown me the gift of friendships that are fruitful. You have also revealed to me the relationships that I have let fall away because I did not tend to them. Give me a heart for those people You bring into my life. Give me insight to know how to nurture and cultivate these connections so that the harvest of my relationships is abundant and brings You joy. Amen.

Take Action

Plant a seed of friendship this week by reaching out to someone. Nurture a seed of friendship you have already planted today by reaching out to connect with a friend or neighbor who has been a part of your life. Let your effort and kindness become light that brings necessary warmth to relationships.

Your Reflections

_____

_____

_____

Guidelines for Godly Living

It is by grace you have been saved, through
faith—and this not from yourselves, it
is the gift of God (Ephesians 2:8).

I've often wondered what God would say to me if I asked Him this question: "God, what would You like me to do in order to receive all that You have willed for my life?" When I read the Bible, I realize that I do receive His response to my question.

Imagine that you can hear God's voice speaking to you. Here are a few things I believe He is saying to us...if we will only listen:

- *Trust Me*—Have faith that I will take care of you. Stop taking back what you have given Me. I am capable of handling all your problems.

- *Talk to Me*—As a loving Dad, I want to hear from you. I want to talk to you in bad times as well as good times. You have a voice like none of My other children; let Me hear it.

- *Be patient*—My plan is not for you to rush, rush, rush. You have many valleys and mountaintops to climb. Trust Me in My timing. My clock is different than your watch.

- *Love yourself*—You are created in My image. I loved you so much that I gave My Son, Jesus, to pay for your sins. If I love you that much, certainly you can love yourself. When you look in the mirror in the morning say, "God, thank You for making me, me."

- *Quit worrying*—Worry causes you to waste your energy

fretting about things that I will take care of for you. Build your trust in Me by giving your worries to Me daily.

- *Put it on My to-do list*—You think your problems or tasks are too minor to give Me, but that is not true. I am waiting for you to share your need with Me.

- *Have faith*—Believe what I have given you in the Scriptures. Even if you can't see Me, I'm right here with you.

Lord, You call me Your child. I belong to You and I am grateful for Your love. Help me to embrace who I am in You and who You are guiding me to become. With faith I give my actions and days and dreams to You. And with faith, I believe all that You say to me, Your daughter. Amen.

Take Action

In a journal or this Reflections section, write down a few questions you have for God. Spend time this week in Scripture seeking His answers. Write down those verses that speak to your heart and your concerns. Consider following the wisdom of this quote from Corrie ten Boom: "I take all my problems each evening and put them at the foot of the cross."

Your Reflections

_____

_____

_____

Conflict Resolution

*Submit to one another out of reverence
for Christ (Ephesians 5:21).*

After a rain storm a little creek flows into a bigger creek, which runs into the larger river, and a few miles downstream it all rushes into an even greater river or maybe even the ocean. What started out small and unassuming becomes big and forceful. That's the flow of intensity that can take place in a quarrel. What starts out as a minor irritation can become a much bigger deal down the line.

If we are spending time growing our faith and deepening our connection to God, we have a greater chance of discerning when we are about to take a slight frustration and turn it into a storm of discontent or anger. Here are six biblical principles of conflict resolution that can help you and me become more sensitive to our words and actions.

1. Psalm 141:3—"Set a guard over my mouth, O LORD; keep watch over the door of my lips." You never have to say "I'm sorry" if you don't say hurtful words.

2. Romans 12:16a (NASB)—"Be of the same mind toward one another." It's so important that you have a history of talking together. You don't have to think alike, but you can come to agreement on what values you will have in the relationship. Agree to disagree even.

3. Romans 12:16b (NASB)—"Do not be haughty in mind, but associate with the lowly. Do not be wise in your own estimation." Paul tells us to be humble when we are in conflict.

4. Romans 12:17 (NASB)—"Never pay back evil for evil to anyone. Respect what is right in the sight of all men." Have empathy for the other person and never respond out of anger.

5. Romans 12:18 (NASB)—"If possible, so far as depends on you, be at peace with all men." Be known as a peacemaker and a listener.

6. Romans 12:19 (NASB)—"Never take your own revenge, beloved, but leave room for the wrath *of God*, for it is written, 'VENGEANCE IS MINE, I WILL REPAY,' says the Lord." God has the final verdict. It is not your job to play God.

Remember that conflict doesn't have to be resolved in one meeting or in one evening. Be patient with others and with yourself as you grow into the role of peacemaker.

Father God, You know that I have trouble with certain people and situations. Give me the strength to respond in compassion and with great patience. I want to understand others better and I want to be an example of Your love, not an obstacle to it. Amen.

Take Action

Where do you have conflict in your life right now? Pray about that situation. Consider how you can approach this person or tension with the heart of a peacemaker. What will that look and feel like?

Your Reflections

_____

_____

_____

Buy One, Get One Free

*Be kind to one another, tender-hearted, forgiving
each other, just as God in Christ also has
forgiven you (Ephesians 4:32 NASB).*

Bob and I are bargain hunters. We like all kinds of discounts. In fact our children wonder about us. We don't like to pay full price for anything. We love the items that have a tag posted, "Buy one, get one free." That's a 50 percent savings. That's quite a deal. But our favorite tag is "Free." Well, to make your day and mine, here are eight gifts that cost us absolutely nothing to give (or receive).

1. *The Gift of Listening.* You must really listen with your eyes and ears. No interrupting, no daydreaming, no checking your phone or glancing at the TV. Just listen.

2. *The Gift of Affection.* Be generous with your hugs or kind words and pats on the back to family members. Let small actions demonstrate the love you have for them.

3. *The Gift of Laughter.* Share funny articles or stories. Call a friend and share about something humorous that happened to you. Your gift will say, "I love to laugh with you."

4. *The Gift of a Written Note.* A simple "I've been thinking of you," or whatever sentiment you want to express, shared in a brief, handwritten note, will matter greatly to the recipient.

5. *The Gift of a Compliment.* A simple and sincere remark can make someone's day. "You look good in that shirt," "I like your new haircut," "What a wonderful report card."

6. *The Gift of a Favor.* Make it a daily goal to do something extra for someone. It will not only make them feel good, but it will also lift your spirits.

7. *The Gift of Solitude.* We live in a very noisy world and our soul needs rest. Be sensitive to those times when you can give the gift of solitude or stillness to others.

8. *The Gift of a Cheerful Disposition.* The easiest way to extend a great, free gift is to extend a kind word to someone. Really, it's not that hard to say "Hello" and "Thank you."

Lord, You are the giver of all gifts! Help me pass along kindness and love in simple ways that show others that I think of them. Encourage me to share with others when I am praying for them as well. In all that I do and all that I am, I want to show people Your bountiful love and mercy. Amen.

Take Action

Choose a different one of these gifts to give to people each day for the next eight days. Then start over! You will experience the joy of giving of your heart and your time in good and godly ways.

Your Reflections

_____

_____

_____

What Makes a Home?

Unless the LORD builds the house, its
builders labor in vain (Psalm 127:1).

As a parent, it is easy to wonder whether we actually have a home or whether we have created more of a stopover place to eat, do laundry, hang around, and sleep. Is it a temporary shelter for your family and for some friends, or do you feel you all are truly grounded in your home and that it is a place that welcomes each member and guest with warmth, hospitality, and acceptance? Do you feel at home in your home?

A true home is a place where people live, grow, laugh, cry, learn, and create memories. A young child, after watching his house burn down, was once quoted as saying, "We still have a home. We just don't have a house to put it in." How perceptive this young child was.

Our homes should be a healing center for the whole family and for anyone who comes along. We don't have to be perfect—just welcoming. We can grow, we can make mistakes, we can laugh, we can cry, we can agree, and we can disagree. All that can happen under one roof!

Home should be a place where happy and sad experiences occur because it is a safe haven for all of life's circumstances to be supported. If we form a shelter from the problems of the world that is a place of love, acceptance, and security, we are building a home for God's work to unfold.

Solomon spoke to this subject in Proverbs 24:3-4. "By wisdom a house is built, and through understanding it is established; through knowledge its rooms are filled with rare and beautiful treasures."

The three most important materials needed to create a godly home are wisdom, understanding, and knowledge. It shouldn't surprise you that these materials are found in the Bible. Just think...as you and I have journeyed together each day, we are building our relationship with God *and* we are gathering the spiritual supplies we need to shape a godly home for ourselves and others.

> God, You are my shelter and my spiritual home. As I come to Your Word for guidance, may I be reaching for the wisdom, under-standing, and knowledge needed to shape a home for those in my life. Wherever I live, You are with me. May my home always be built on Your foundation and may it always have a door that is open wide in Your name. Amen.

Take Action

Look around your home and consider all the ways you do or you can extend hospitality to your family and to those who visit. If you shape spaces that are welcoming to you, they will welcome in others too. Let this be a home that glorifies the Lord.

Your Reflections

_____

_____

_____

Pray for a Friend

I have not stopped giving thanks for you,
remembering you in my prayers (Ephesians 1:16).

One of the ways to be a supportive friend is to pray for them when they are going through a difficult time in their life. The apostle Paul wrote prayers to encourage other believers.

- "And this is my prayer: that your love may abound still more and more in knowledge and depth of insight, so that you may be able to discern what is best and may be pure and blameless until the day of Christ, filled with the fruit of righteousness that comes through Jesus Christ—to the glory and praise of God" (Philippians 1:9-11).

- "Since the day we heard about you, we have not stopped praying for you and asking God to fill you with the knowledge of his will through all spiritual wisdom and understanding" (Colossians 1:9).

- "We constantly pray for you, that our God may count you worthy of his calling, and that by his power he may fulfill every good purpose of yours and every act prompted by your faith" (2 Thessalonians 1:11).

Praying for others is a privilege and a big responsibility. I have a spiral notebook and I write down the person's name listed along with a note about what the need is. When the Lord has answered that request I put a check mark to the right of the request. Some names have been on the ledger for some time. With chronic problems they are ongoing.

An occasional note or telephone call is an encouragement to your friends. When a friend of ours passed away, his daughter told us that her father had kept notes of encouragement that we had sent over the years. Don't ever underestimate the importance of following your heart to share inspiration and kindness with others.

Lead me, Lord. Direct my thoughts toward the people in my life who need a word of cheer or a note of encouragement. Give me a heart that is sensitive to the needs of others so that I might be quick to pray for those needs and be mindful of them when I have a chance to extend generosity of spirit in any form. I want to have a heart for Your children and to act out of love. It is a privilege to be a friend to another. Amen.

Take Action

Reflect on the following quote from Sir H. Davy and then plan a few simple kindnesses to extend to others this week. "Life is made up, not of great sacrifices or duties, but of little things, in which smiles, and kindnesses, and small obligations, given habitually, are what win and preserve the heart and secure comfort."

Your Reflections

_____

_____

_____

Why Go to Church?

Let us consider how we may spur one another on
toward love and good deeds (Hebrews 10:24).

Why go to church? A lot of nonbelievers ask this question. I think a lot of Christians even ask this. People start to wonder if going to church is a waste of time or at least something on their schedule that could easily be removed to make room for other activities and commitments. After all, our weekends can become full pretty quickly with soccer games, brunch with friends, house and yard chores, and errands we don't get to during the work week.

That is all true. And I admit that it can be tough to keep the commitment to church all the time, but there is great value in being faithful in this area of your spiritual discipline and your family's spiritual growth. And where are you going to be challenged and lifted up if not church?

The truest perspective to have about church is, however, not about what we get out of it, but why we are there to begin with. Your Sunday service is a devoted time to give back to God for what He's done for you. We can lift up His name and our voice in songs of praise. We show our love and adoration for all He has given and all that He has done in our lives. That is the power of church.

Bob and I have found that church provides a wonderful support group to help us better live our lives. During my bout with cancer, our strongest prayer support came from our church family. They were the ones who offered meals, helped to sit with me when I had my chemo, helped us in our office work, ran errands, and returned calls for us.

Connecting with a church is about Christ and then the body of

Christ. Our relationship to our Lord and to His people is meant to give us strength and courage. This time of fellowship and praising God also reminds us that we are not alone in this life or in our faith journey. Together we can conquer and accomplish amazing things for God's kingdom. We need the church to make us more faithful people.

God, I need You and I need Your people. Help me follow through with my commitment to go to church and to be an active part of the body of Christ. Direct my heart so that my time in worship is truly about worshipping You. Thank You for the gift of community and for the holiness of every day that I walk with You, God. Amen.

Take Action

Think about your attitude toward church and your perspective about what church is in light of today's devotion. Do you enter church with a heart of praise and worship? Or is your heart weighed down with a perspective that is limited to your needs or concerns that day? Truly worship the Lord this Sunday and see how that changes everything!

Your Reflections

_____

_____

_____

There Will Be Tears All Night

Be merciful to me, LORD, for I am faint; heal me, O LORD, heal me, for my bones are in agony (Psalm 6:2).

In this psalm, David is asking God how long his suffering will last. He cries out, "Pity me, O Lord, for I am weak; heal me for my body is sick." I know a little of the feelings behind David's petition to God; I had the same utterances in my life when my doctor announced that I had cancer. Little did I know how sick I was going to be, or the long journey Bob and I would be traveling.

There were days when we didn't know if I had another day left in my body. The doctors and nurses certainly did not know. During those many times of uncertainty, we claimed Psalm 30:5, "Weeping may last for the night, but a shout of joy comes in the morning (NASB)." It seemed that there were many days, weeks, and months that we had long nights of weeping.

Today we would be so different if we had not gone through that period in our lives. Bob and I bombarded God several times a day, asking Him to deliver me from this prison of illness. At times it didn't seem like He was even listening to our pleas. Often we were discouraged, but we hung our faith onto the character of God and all of His promises.

After several years, we could see that God was turning the ship around from illness to recovery. It has now been a long time since cancer invaded our lives, but we have been able to shout for joy for what God, the medical profession, and medicine have done for me. Where once I lay helpless on a bed or couch, I now experience a significant level of good health. During the past dark days, we never could have imagined the quality of life that I have today.

God acts beyond our ability to understand and thank goodness for that. God is good—all the time. Be assured that God has heard your prayers and cries.

> Lord, I bring my physical and emotional wounds to You today. I ask for Your healing and grace. I trust You with all of my life. Even when I stand in the darkness of uncertainty, I do see Your light and I believe in it. Your presence saves me from discouragement and my hope in You carries me this day. Amen.

Take Action

If you are facing a time of darkness or doubt right now, go to God frequently. He will not tire of you asking for His guidance and light. Lift up your hurts right now, friend.

Your Reflections

_____

_____

_____

Find Favor in the Eyes of God

*Noah found favor in the eyes of the LORD...Noah did
everything just as God commanded him (Genesis 6:8,22).*

Every day we see in the paper or read in emails or posts stories about individuals who are being honored by the world. On and on it goes. People finding favor with people or seeking it. We can look at those receiving praise, accolades, or "likes" on Facebook and become a bit jealous. We all like to get a vote of confidence now and then, don't we?

But have you ever thought how much more meaningful it is to have God find favor with you? This is one of the blessings of our faith. We don't need the world's praises to feel good about ourselves. We have the Creator of the world loving us! I stand in awe when I think of God finding favor in me, but He does. Only through His marvelous grace are we able to come to Him face-to-face.

In the story of Noah, we find that he too lived during a time when the world was full of sin. I guess the intensity of stresses and temptations in society hasn't changed much over the centuries. Yet even though Noah was surrounded by all of this wickedness, he strived to live a godly life. His life was pleasing to God even during those evil days.

Noah didn't find favor because of his individual goodness but through his personal faith in God. We are also judged according to the same standard—our personal faith and obedience to God's Word. My daily prayer is that my family and I will be worthy of the goodness God so richly bestows upon us.

Even though Noah was upright and blameless before God, he wasn't perfect. God recognized that Noah's life reflected a genuine faith, not always a perfect faith. When we come to God and admit we have fallen short of His standards and admit we are sinners—that is pleasing to God. Then we find the grace of God and that is sufficient.

Just like Noah, we might be surrounded by troubles that are more likely to pull us away from God than push us toward Him, but our heart will lead us to God's presence. In His grace, we will find the only favor we will ever need.

> Lord, I pray to have a heart and life that please You. Your favor gives me my value. I don't need the world's applause to know that I am a worthy daughter of the King. Your grace makes me worthy. Your love makes me whole. I want for nothing. Amen.

Take Action

The next time you feel less than because you have not been noticed or rewarded by those around you, consider where your true value lies.

Your Reflections

_____

_____

_____

His Name Is Wonderful

For to us a child is born, to us a son is given, and the government will be on his shoulders. And he will be called Wonderful Counselor, Mighty God, Everlasting Father, Prince of Peace (Isaiah 9:6).

In Isaiah's verse we find six separate adjectives and nouns to express the character of the Son of God—Jesus. There is something so powerful and so tender in the names of God, that I cannot do anything but praise Him.

Our thoughts today can turn to the positive, even if we face trials, because we are able to look to the goodness and wonder of the Lord. We can claim relationship with our Wonderful Counselor, Mighty God, Everlasting Father, and Prince of Peace.

He is Almighty God who parted the Red Sea, raised Lazarus from the dead, fed the hungry, healed the lame, and forgave the sinners—even those who betrayed Him.

There is nothing that He can't do.

God lives today in our hearts. His power is a miracle in our lives. And His peace is for us to experience. God didn't promise that we wouldn't have valleys in our lives, but He did give us peace to walk with Him. To be sure, life will bring sorrow, broken hearts, health problems, financial difficulties, and much more that could challenge our convictions. But God doesn't leave us there in the midst of the trouble. He makes a way for us and we can follow Him through anything.

Take your problems and worries of today and lay them at the foot of the cross. Give them to Jesus. Walk away and don't take them back. How often have you surrendered a need to the Lord and then tried to resolve it in your own power the next day? Let's really surrender our lives and needs to God. Let's experience the life and peace of Jesus completely.

There is just something about that name—Jesus.

Wonderful Counselor, You are my guide and my God. When my steps falter, You are there to help me stand upright and to walk forward in Your way. You know my heart and my flaws and You still love me. When I cannot see beyond my burdens, direct my eyes to Your face. When I cannot speak of anything except my troubles, direct my tongue to praise Your every name. Amen.

Take Action

Pray to God using the names in today's verse: Wonderful Counselor, Mighty God, Everlasting Father, and Prince of Peace. As you pray, embrace that aspect of God's character with pure joy. And when you go about your day, think about leaning on God's faithful character in new ways.

Your Reflections

_____

_____

_____

God Is with You

I have called you by name; you are mine. When you go
through deep waters, I will be with you. When you go
through rivers of difficulty, you will not drown. When
you walk through the fire of oppression, you will not
be burned up; the flames will not consume you. For
I am the LORD, your God (Isaiah 43:1-3 NLT).

In today's verse, notice that Isaiah says "when," not "if" about going through rivers of difficulty. Sooner or later in life all of us will go through deep troubles. How will you respond when this day comes to you or a member of your family? If we are blessed with an abundance of years, we will eventually

- pass through deep waters
- wade through the rivers
- walk through the fire

Isaiah states:

- You will not drown.
- You will not be burned up.
- You will not be consumed by the flames.

His promise is:

- The rivers aren't sweeping over me.
- God is calling me by name and I will fear no evil.

Your attitude will determine your latitude in life. There is something about faith and hope that lets us experience these downturns in life as bearable. You may not physically survive these events here on earth, but your eternal perspective will give you a peace as you go through these valleys.

The apostle Paul prayed to God three times to heal the thorn in his side, but God didn't see fit to heal him. God answered back, "My grace is sufficient for you, for my power is made perfect in weakness." With this Paul said to himself, "I will boast all the more gladly about my weaknesses, so that Christ's power may rest on me" (2 Corinthians 12:9). Paul understood that his need made him more dependent upon God for all things.

My friend, your journey of spending time with God has been a journey of growing dependence on God. The rewards are great: faith in His promises, trust in your Savior, light in the darkness, comfort in your need, and hope for your future.

Father God, You are my light. You are my hope. You are my Lord today and tomorrow. Amen.

Take Action

Spend time in prayer today thanking God for His presence. Continue your new habit of talking with God, studying His Word, and embracing His promises all the days of your life.

Your Reflections

_____

_____

_____

About the Author

Emilie Barnes is an accomplished, respected home organizer who has devoted her life to serving and encouraging her family and countless women. She has authored more than 70 books including *If Teacups Could Talk, 15 Minutes Alone with God, 101 Ways to Clean Out the Clutter*, and *More Hours in My Day*.

She and her husband, Bob Barnes, founded More Hours in My Day ministry in 1980 and spent 30 years ministering, speaking, and writing books. They have been married for 60 years and together celebrate a legacy of two children, five grandchildren, and three great-grandchildren.

Visit www.emiliebarnes.com for more information about Emilie's books and the continuing ministry of More Hours in My Day.

More Books by Emilie
and Bob Barnes

Bob & Emilie Barnes

*101 Ways to Love Your
    Grandchildren*
15-Minute Devotions for Couples
Good Manners for Today's Kids
Little Book of Manners for Boys, A
Simple Secrets Couples Should Know
Together Moments for Couples

Bob Barnes

15 Minutes Alone with God for Men
500 Handy Hints for Every Husband
5-Minute Bible Workouts for Men
5-Minute Faith Builders for Men
Five Minutes in the Bible for Men
*Old Guy's Guide to
    Living Young, An*
One Minute Alone with God for Men
What Makes a Man Feel Loved

Emilie Barnes

101 Ways to Clean Out the Clutter
15 Minutes Alone with God
15 Minutes of Peace with God
15 Minutes with God for Grandma
15-Minute Organizer, The
*365 Things Every Woman Should
    Know*
365 Ways to Organize Everything

*500 Time-Saving Hints for Every
    Woman*
An Invitation to Tea
Emilie's Creative Home Organizer
Five Minutes in the Bible for Women
Good Manners for Every Occasion
Good Manners in Minutes
Heal My Heart, Lord
I Need Your Strength, Lord
In the Stillness of Quiet Moments
Journey Through Cancer, A
Keep It Simple for Busy Women
Let's Have a Tea Party!
Little Book of Manners
Meet Me Where I Am, Lord
Minute Meditations for Busy Moms
*Minute Meditations for Healing &
    Hope*
More Faith in My Day
More Hours in My Day
Quick-Fix Home Organizer, The
Quiet Moments Alone with God
Simple Secrets to a Beautiful Home
Survival for Busy Women
Tea Lover's Devotional, The
Twelve Teas® of Inspiration, The
Walk with Me Today, Lord
What Makes a Woman Feel Loved
You Are My Hiding Place, Lord
Youniquely Woman

To learn more about Harvest House books and
to read sample chapters, visit our website:

www.harvesthousepublishers.com

HARVEST HOUSE PUBLISHERS
EUGENE, OREGON